M000283872

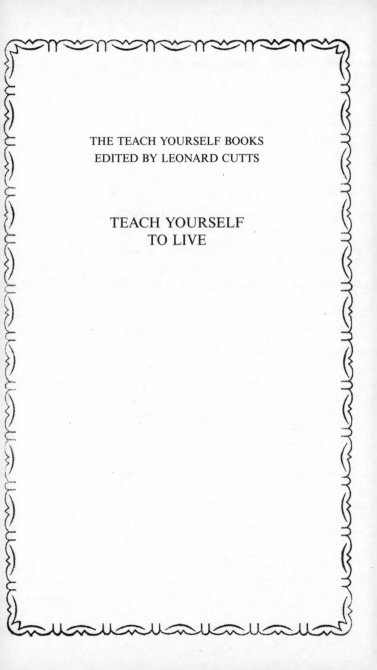

THE TEACH YOURSELF BOOKS
EDITED BY LEONARD CUTTS

TEACH YOURSELF
TO LIVE

In the same series

———

Teach Yourself Bird Watching
Teach Yourself Cycling
Teach Yourself Good Manners
Teach Yourself to Fly

Teach® Yourself

TEACH YOURSELF

TO LIVE

By
C. G. L. DU CANN

CONTENTS

PREFACE

For the present year in which I write, England's national bill for formal education, central and local, is no less than £392,000,000.

But it is safe to say that not a single pound of that vast sum of money will be spent in teaching anyone the fundamental art of how to live to the best advantage. Almost every other conceivable branch of knowledge will be taught. Yet not the one subject which concerns us all more than any other and which should cover and include everything that it is really necessary and desirable for us to know.

A curious fact, truly! Nothing in the curriculum of schools and universities is of more importance than the art, science, and business of life. Everything else in the whole field of human knowledge is, after all, merely subsidiary and ancillary to living itself.

Perhaps it is because we are all conscious, teachers no less than others, of the profound, and indeed abysmal, ignorance of all of us on that great subject, that we shrink from trying to teach what we probably believe in our hearts to be incommunicable. Where Philosophy and Religion tread with doubt and fear, mere Worldly Wisdom may justly fear to rush in. Some of course will say that Life itself teaches us how to live. This is quite true. But through what processes of trial and error, what pain and suffering, and how often too late for our peace and our good! From much of this a helping hand and a warning voice might have saved us, for Experience, though the best of teachers, is often an expensive and cruel one.

Indeed, formal education does not get us very far. No University turns out a Shakespeare, a Dickens, a Bernard Shaw, a Newton, or an Einstein, a Beethoven or a Mozart. It is their own lives and their own natures that give such men the extra and original something which we call genius, and which raises them above their fellows to the enrichment of us all.

Progress in science and mechanics, owing to formal education it is true, has been stupendous. In the immediate past of my own lifetime, I have seen such miracles of new invention as the motor-car, the ever-faster aircraft, the radio, televison, the atom and hydrogen bombs, supersonic speed, and the hope of interplanetary travel. But what progress have I seen in spirituality, morality, intellectuality, or in the art of great and gracious living to the best advantage in my lifetime?

It is devastating to have to answer: None.

People are not wiser or better to-day than they were in the days of ancient Greece or Rome. (Indeed, it might be argued quite plausibly that they are less wise and less good). For one cannot imagine Marcus Aurelius or Jesus Christ accepting as inevitable such horrors as Hiroshima and Nagasaki, or the morality of nations which are preparing for the lunatic and diabolic Atom Warfare of the future which is to spare none. This is not human progress. It is human regression indeed—that we should sink below the spiritual and intellectual state of the ancients.

And if people are not better or wiser than of old, they are certainly no more effective or efficient in the art of living to the best advantage. Classical literature shows that plainly enough.

All this is the more reason for individual striving to be wiser and better. To live to the best advantage, whether at work or play, whether at home or abroad, whether in solitude or in multitude, from infancy to old age, at all times and in all circumstances, is surely no ignoble ideal. To live the fullest life, to develop one's self to one's full capacity, is surely what we should aspire to and strive to do. So imperfect is the human machine of body, mind, and spirit under the long and varied stress and strain of daily living, that this is not always attainable. None the less, we may reach our highest and best at times and at all times not fall too far below it.

In this great enterprise, one can only attain fullness of life by living and not by reading about it. Still, a book can help to a varying degree, dependent upon what a reader brings to it. It may stimulate or suggest. It may inspire or inspirit. It may gain assent or provoke dissent. It may be valuable in other ways. I hope this present book may help those who study it, especially youthful questioners of life, and that, at least, it may interest all who pay its author the compliment of reading its lessons in the great art of effective living.

—C. du C.

CHAPTER I

TENURE AND CONDITIONS OF EXISTENCE

1. Yourself

F ACE the facts of life. Few do. Few dare. This is the first and most important thing in order to make the best of yourself and your life and in order to live to the best advantage in this terrestial world.

When people talk of knowing the facts of life they usually mean nothing more than knowing about sex. It is true that sex is a fact of life, a fundamental fact, for many human beings the fundamental fact in one form or another for most of their life. But sex is, in spite of common misinterpretations of Freudian doctrine, far from being the whole of the facts of life. It is but one. And only for a period is it even the over-riding one in any human life.

What are life-facts? The first is Yourself. The second is Existence. The third is the limited nature of Yourself and your Existence. That is to say YOU EXIST ON TERMS. Those three things are inexorable, desperate facts unwilled by you and which you are completely powerless to alter.

Realise the limitations which these three facts of life impose on you. Otherwise you do not get a clear perspective of the problem of living in this world.

Take the first fact—Yourself. The current cant of

our day and generation—this being the era of the common man—talks and writes as though You, Mr. Everyman, have illimitable powers which by education and will-power in a properly organised State and other magical and miraculous nostrums can achieve the height of imaginable well-being and happiness. But you are not illimitable. By heredity and the mere fact of being a man or woman, you are severely, and even perhaps cruelly, limited. The sins and virtues of your fathers are visited upon you, unjust though that be. You are as truly imprisoned within your physical and mental self as if you were captive and held in Dartmoor or Sing-Sing.

At the same time it is perfectly true that by education (using that word in its widest, and including its extra-scholastic, sense), by courage, energy, and determination; by pursuing unflinchingly some aim and purpose in life, you can perform miracles with Yourself. Yet there is a limit which says, "Thus far and no farther", like Canute to the sea-waves, and with more certainty.

For instance, your physical self may be capable—your body being the inherited thing it is—of growing to a maximum of (say) five feet ten inches. Lead a healthy well-nourished existence under the most favourable conditions during the years of growth, and you may attain that maximum. Live in an unhealthy slum and be ill-nourished under unfavourable conditions during that crucial period, and you may end by being five feet seven, or less.

But do what you will, you and your particular body cannot attain a height of over five feet ten inches.

Others can. You cannot. Though you take thought for ever, your body will not do more than it can—by birth.

So much for your body. What of your mind? Alas! it is subject to the same iron law. If you are not a Beethoven, a Michael Angelo, a Shakespeare, a Newton, or an Einstein, all the Universities and studying in the world will not make you one.

Formal education, still better the informal education that is self-achieved; experience; exercise; and other facts, can immeasurably improve your mind as healthy eating and drinking and adequate care and exercise can improve your body. But there are limits to this mental-improvement process. If you are born tone-deaf (and many are) nothing will make you a musician. You cannot make literary minds into mathematical ones or engineering ones. Some minds are born incurably specialist. Others can manage a bit of everything. The tortoise-mind can never become a hare-mind—but it may outdistance the hare for all that.

This truth is so obviously true that even in popular parlance, the differing calibre of human minds is recognised by the word "gifted". There are minds with a distinct "gift" for words, or form, or music, or mathematics, engineering, and the rest. Mozart was an accomplished musician, John Stuart Mill an accomplished literary student even in infancy.

Recognise, then, that both in body and mind You are You, and not a better or worse Anybody Else. You are limited by Yourself. You can make the Best of Yourself—or fall short of that very desirable consummation so devoutly to be wished and pursued. But you cannot go beyond that.

How wise is the Greek axiom of Socrates: "Know Thyself." This has been called the beginning of wisdom. It is so, indeed. And the first step in knowing oneself is to know one's own limitations as well as one's powers.

Depressing? Not a bit of it. No more depressing than a cold shower-bath is depressing. At first it may shock. But in a while it is exhilarating. You know where you are—exactly. You are no longer befogged and bewildered by false and misleading Illusion about yourself and life—like most people.

In Matthew Arnold's phrase you "see life steadily and see it whole". And yourself, too.

What are you to do with this limited Self of yours? You are of course to make the most of it, in its own interests as well as the world's. (If you are religious, you will say this is your duty to God, your Neighbour, and your Self).

As this Self is a body and a mind, not merely one or the other, you have a twofold task. You must take care, great care, of both. For they are all you have and are. Sacrifice neither one to the other, as athletes and students often do. Cultivate them both to the height of their powers so that each functions to your best advantage. That, and that only, is the whole problem of life.

So much for the You.

2. Existence

Do you ever think about existence in general?

Probably not. Yet you had better. After all, you do exist and can no other, as Martin Luther once said.

Existence is a mysterious thing. You come into it not of your own volition. You will certainly go from it when your time comes, not of your own volition. And there you are.

You share the gift of life with plants, animals, and your fellow human beings. And all of these things that have life are subject to the same laws. You think yourself highly superior to the grass of the field, the birds of the air, the fish of the sea, the beasts of the forest. But science teaches you that in many ways you are not superior, being bound as you are by the same iron band of existence in this physical material world.

Of course in some ways, man is definitely superior. At any rate, he has established dominion over the others, and success is always held, by human standards, to imply superiority.

There is a well-known saying: "A man must live". Precisely. In that saying everything about existence is summed up and said. Willy-nilly you must live. For no better reason—which is the best of reasons—than that you are alive. Like a clock wound-up, you must go on until you run down.

Your existence, too, is a fact that has to be faced by others no less than yourself. As long as you live, you count. When you are dead, you don't. Unless you are an exceptional being, that is; when, being an exceptional being, you may live in the hearts and minds and lives of others.

You may wish to attain that second existence (often

exaggeratedly spoken of as "immortality"). If you are so avidly ambitious as to desire Fame, which Milton called "the last infirmity of noble mind", you are not debarred from it and may even be helped towards it, by living to the best ádvantage.

Your present existence, however, may well be as much as you wish to manage.

Though you could not begin life by your own volition, you can end it if you will. (Far be it from me, however, to suggest that you should.) The Ancients, and in particular the Ancient Romans, prided themselves on both the ability and the will to commit suicide. They thought it a noble thing that a man should, if life were intolerable, or dishonourable, or if he had had enough of it, deliberately end his existence by that man's own act. In more modern times, some Japanese have thought the same thing.

But modern Western folk in general do not think along those lines. They believe that life is to be lived to its end. This is also the teaching of the Christian faith, as well as the law of England, which regards suicide, and even attempted suicide, as a criminal act.

Existence, then, is to be continued. Your existence anyhow is constantly, too constantly, threatened. War, disease, accident, nay even Time itself, the very stuff of which life is made, and even you, yourself, by your appetites, over-indulged, threaten it. To preserve it you may well realise the necessity of taking pains to do so.

To probe the mystery of existence *qua* existence, is fascinating. This, however, is the work of poets, philosophers, mystics, metaphysicians, theologians, and similar seers. The business of ordinary practical persons, doing the everyday work of the world, is less to speculate upon existence than to exist and make their existence fruitful. This is not beyond the lowest, or above the highest, of us.

And in order to exist fruitfully, grasp the trite truth that the stuff of existence is Time. That is to say, seconds, minutes, hours, days, weeks, months, and years.

"I know all that" you perhaps exclaim impatiently. Well, then, act as if you know it, not as if you merely know about it. Time consists of seconds. When you catch a train by a second then you do really know it! But generally you do not—none of us do—realise imaginatively and usefully, the stuff of Time. If we did, we should use time more wisely. Time is to be used like money; to be spent, in general, to advantage, and sometimes a little is to be wasted. But, like one's money, one's time should never be habitually frittered away, nor should it be lost in large and fruitless expenditures, bringing no harvest.

Look at this stuff of existence as it really is. A small ephemeral period of little, if any, importance, to all others, even of your own day and generation, but of terrible and utter importance to yourself. This tiny fragment of your life is sandwiched between aeons of of Time Past and aeons of Time Future. That is all you possess, little in itself but greater than Eternity to you. Just as a pound in your pocket is worth more to you than millions in the Government's—a remark stemming from one first uttered by Sancho Panza in *Don Quixote*.

Now once you grip the reality of existence—that it is time and so little time at that—you will avoid many pitfalls and errors. Also you will realise that existence is a gift to be used, and to continue to be used, until it is suddenly withdrawn as it is from all sentient things by death. The paths of virtue and wisdom, like Gray's path of glory and indeed all other human paths, lead but to the grave. That fact makes it more important to live, work, and hope.

3. Terms and Conditions

The gift of life is not absolute. Far from it. We have already seen it is subject to terms and conditions not of your choice, nor even of your agreement. These are, perforce, imposed upon you. You cannot, as the lawyers say, contract out of them.

Like the laws of the Medes and Persians, these laws of life "altereth not". And, first, there are such terms and conditions as are imposed on all mankind, which you must abide by whether you will or not. One comfort you have in this tyrannic state of affairs: the closer you abide by them the more to your advantage.

These terms and conditions are plain enough. In physical life they are such as the law of periodic sleep, the law of eating and drinking, the law of breathing, the law of bodily and mental exercise, to name a few of the most obviously important.

Most people take these physical necessities for granted and "manage somehow". They leave it to outraged Nature to redress the balance. This is a grievous mistake.

For while it is quite true that if you keep awake for

a couple or more days and nights, Nature will force you to sleep, even perhaps standing, this is not good for you. Or if you eat or drink to excess, Nature will take charge and make you sick, so that you cannot continue. But for such redress Nature makes you pay.

Better keep the law. For there is this difference between Nature's laws and the laws of man: Nature always finds out your infraction of her laws in its very committal and always automatically punishes without even waiting for the completion of the crime against her ordinances.

Let us look at these stringent—or rather inexorable —terms. Everyone knows them: they are the common-places of all life. But few look at them beyond the extent that their imposition forces people to look at them. Yet your lease of life is held subject to them.

First: you have no freehold in perpetuity of your life. It lasts some 70 years, more or less, as the Psalmist noted. You can shorten it by foolish living: you may lengthen it by wise living. But not greatly. It is a mere leasehold.

Second: a great part of it is deducted from your conscious ruling of it. You may sleep away as much as a third of it (or even more) if you are foolish enough to do so. Also, there is the semi-consciousness of helpless infancy. There may even be a second childhood in old age. There is also an inevitable wastage in trifling and the like.

It may be reckoned that you do well if you actually enjoy in grand total 35 to 40 years of conscious, purposeful, self-ruled existence. To the young that sounds a great deal. Older people realise that it is pitifully little. But if you are to make the most of it you had better imaginatively realise these truly terrible limitations of your conscious being.

About infancy you can do nothing. Nor need you. Others provide for that, from the necessity of the case. Reflecting upon that strange circumstance may lead you to see that you start your working-life in debt to others. That is a fair statement of the case, is it not?

But old age you can, should, and must, provide for. True, these are days of Old-Age Pensions. But this does not detract from the plain duty of each of us to recognise that old-age may, and probably will, come with all the disability that age entails, and to realise the paramount necessity of providing for that possibly evil day. Nor is it desirable to work to the very end of life, "to die in harness" as many men boast. Nature intends a rest towards the end, as after the beginning, of life.

Every young man and young woman "knows" that he or she will grow old. In a way they do know it. But old age—for them—seems so faint and far off and incredible that they do not really know that at all. They feel that the aged are a different race, nay, a different order of being, from themselves—even while they "know" they are not. Besides, they secretly think there is plenty of time.

There is not plenty of time. There is very little time. The aged realise that. Sometimes they feel and say that "life has gone like a flash". Before they realised its potentialities!

Disraeli once cynically said: "Youth is a blunder,

Manhood a struggle; Old Age a regret." That is not mere cynicism. There is a lot of truth in it. And one of the blunders of youth is non-preparation for old age.

Old age requires comfort, even luxury. It requires a sufficiency of hard cash. It needs an interest in life—something to live for, something to do, be, and think. It is too late to think about providing these things once old-age has come. They are the harvest from youth and maturity.

Third: Infancy and old age are not the only certain disabilities. Unless you are extremely lucky (you may be) you will meet with such misfortunes as illness or accident. These possibilities also need prevision and provision. Do not rule them out altogether. Or rely entirely on State-aid. State-aid is never enough.

Finally, Solon, the wisest man of Greece, uttered the immortal advice: "Look to the End." There is no need to dwell upon death, for most of life death is best forgotten. Nevertheless, it should be realised as this puts the events of life into proper perspective.

Such are some obvious inexorable terms and conditions imposed by Nature on your life as a member of the human race.

These, however, are not all. There are terms imposed on you as an individual. And it is of the highest importance to your welfare that you find out what these are. This truth is little recognised.

Each of us is highly idiosyncratic. We have what doctors call a constitution. Learn what you can do and what you cannot, what you like and what you dislike, what is meat and drink for your body and your mind and what is poison or useless to them. Never—whatever you do—struggle against the laws of your own being. It is as foolish as a violet trying to be a rose, or a frog trying to be a bull. And it is done by human beings, to their detriment and sorrow, more often than you would dream.

Live within the limits of yourself is a good living rule.

Above all, do not wrest yourself from your own being to copy others or to conform unnecessarily to their conventions or opinions. Champagne has a high reputation, but why drink champagne if you really prefer ginger-beer? In that case it is not champagne to you. Do not struggle to like it, you will probably be defeated anyway, and there is nothing but extra expense in attaining a liking for champagne.

How rigid are the terms imposed by Nature on you as an individual you will understand if you look at yourself in a full-length mirror! The colour of your eyes, the shape of your nose, the texture of your skin, your physique, and so on—there they are, pre-destined and beyond your control.

Do you really think that it is not the same with your mind? That it has not its own cast of temper, its own strengths and weaknesses, its capacities and non-capacities? Of course it has.

You may improve the body and improve the mind, and rightly you will strive to those ends. But get it well into your head: there are limits which all your striving cannot transcend. There is no need to worry about that. You are you to make the best of yourself, and your best, by the fact of its being that, will be very good indeed.

Now, besides these limitations, there are others imposed not by Nature, not by your individuality, but by convention. You live amongst your fellows. And there is a communal standard to which you must conform if you are to live tolerably.

For instance; take clothing. You must clothe yourself willy-nilly. And if you are a man you must dress as a man and if you are a woman you must dress as a woman (even in these days when women's dress often apes men's). These laws of mere convention are, in general, as binding upon you as the laws of Nature or yourself. They are not to be broken with impunity at all times and in all places, as you very well know.

But these laws of mere convention are, of course, not absolute. You can be even a nudist or a sea-bather at the proper times and places, for example. Conventions have not the inexorable rigidity of the other terms and conditions upon which you exist.

Such are the terms and conditions upon which you hold your frail but tenacious tenure of life.

Whether or not they are good enough is a moot point. But whether or not, you cannot alter them. Eternal life may be better than temporary life. Invulnerability to disease, accident, and all the ills that flesh is heir to, may be better than any present human vulnerability. Not to need sleep or sustenance or defecation would be very convenient. Self-reproduction without a partner might save a lot of complications. And so on. One can easily imagine a host of simplifications and improvements in the human machine.

But you cannot make them. The pattern for well or ill is fixed. You can only ignore that fact at your peril or recognise it to your advantage.

All this is so obvious that you would think that everyone, for his or her own sake, would recognise this state of human affairs.

The exact contrary is the case, however. People live, or rather boggle the business of living, by ignoring, forgetting, or only half-apprehending, the fundamental facts of human life and their own being.

They do not sleep to advantage. They eat and drink to their damnation (as religious folk say). They hunger and thirst after trying to be someone else, quite other than themselves. They strain themselves to unhappiness and despair, against the laws of their own being, kicking against the pricks. So they lose their lives in futility and frustration. So they are ineffectual, ill, and unhappy from their foolish way of failing to live according to the laws of Nature and their own being.

And all this comes from never having given an hour's, nay, probably not a moment's, thought to Life itself and the terms and conditions upon which they hold it.

Once you face up to the realities of it, Life takes on richer and fuller meaning and significance. It is no longer an uncharted chaos. It is seen clearly, free from the mists of Illusion. It becomes something (although its mystery remains unsolved) that you can follow and understand as being regulated by laws that are ascertainable and ascertained. And you, by doing so, are by that one fact, an exceptional person —ahead of the rest who have failed to apprehend Life and themselves.

Let us now recapitulate what we have learned from this Chapter.

1.   Face the facts—all the facts—of life.

2.   The facts are comprised in "You Exist on Terms".

3.   You are limited by heredity in body and mind and yet within those limitations you can make the most and best of both.

4.   To know Yourself as the Greek Socrates taught is the beginning of wisdom for yourself.

5.   Self-cultivation of both body and mind to the height of their powers is the answer to the whole problem of life.

6.   Life is to be lived as well as speculated about.

7.   The stuff of Life is Time. Life is a leasehold for a limited term of years, not a freehold in perpetuity, and its inescapable physical and mental terms and conditions are imposed upon you. Realise them. Look to the beginning, middle, and end.

8.   Some of these terms are imposed on the whole of humanity and others on us as individuals.

9.   Lesser terms are imposed by convention.

10.   People blunder in life by not apprehending and living by the laws of life and their own selves.

11.   Master these laws. Then life becomes clear and meaningful to you, yourself, an exceptional person able to live to the best advantage.

CHAPTER II

PERSONALITY: OR, WHAT YOU ARE

1. Personal Capital

L ET us now look a little more closely at the much-misunderstood mystery of Personality or What you are.

"This is an age of cant," as Stendhal, the great French author, reported as being one of Lord Byron's great sayings. And about few things is more current cant talked than about "personalities". Take Dr. Johnson's advice and clear your mind of cant—on this subject as on others.

In popular talk, personality is a special something, a something to be found only amongst the *elite*, amongst geniuses, tycoons, film-stars, and the like. Not amongst the humble and obscure. If such folk are distinctive they are merely "characters" or oddities, or eccentrics. Or at best, they are ordinary, commonplace persons.

Now the truth is that everyone, however self-effacing, however lowly, however negative, possesses a personality. It may be unpronounced. It may be modest, retiring, or almost negligible. It may be self-effacing or self-sacrificing. It may be of little value or interest to the world. But still it exists and it exists in its own right of existence. Whether others recognise it or not, whether they appreciate or not, it is still there.

A thing indeed to be reckoned with by its possessor and the rest of the world. This is true, whether the personality be a strong and formidable one like that (say) of Milton's Satan, or such a reality as Hitler or Stalin, or an almost negligible one like Mrs. Charles Dickens or the very humblest of human creatures inhabiting London.

For personality is not what you seem to others—a vulgar error. It is not even what you seem to yourself. It is what you, in fact, are.

To use another word, less debased by popular use, it is your individuality. The sum total of it. Or, put another way: what you have in yourself.

And what is this? What have you? Do you really know? Have you even tried to find out—exactly and truthfully?

Let us make the effort to find out, here and now. That effort may be valuable. Indeed, self-knowledge is always valuable. Certainly it will be interesting. For nothing is more interesting than oneself—to oneself!

Goethe, the famous German, asked that question "What have we?" And answered it. "What have we in life but our courage and energy and will-power?" he demanded of his friend, Eckermann.

At first sight this is a pregnant saying. But it is incomplete, a half-truth. As far as it goes it is magnificent as a summary of the mind and its governor, the will. But it takes no account of the other partner, the body, which for good or ill, we equally have in life.

Even as a statement of mental possessions, too, Goethe's answer is incomplete, for even the youngest child has acquired (by the exercise of those qualities) a body of mental wealth, a great treasure.

Look at yourself keenly. Calculate your personal capital. It may be divided into three distinct divisions conveniently, though you are, like the Trinity in theology, three-in-one and essentially a Unity.

There is the body, mind, and—something more important than either. Religious people call it the soul, or the spirit; some philosophers call it the Ego or governing part, others call it simply The Will. This last term will do for us. For its name does not matter: what does matter is that you should recognise its reality and its separate existence.

2. The Will

Your body's importance is plain enough—every ache, pain, or illness or physical discomfort, however trifling, reminds you of that. Your mind's importance is also clear—every need to remember, to learn, to understand, reminds you that it counts. The importance—I almost wrote super-importance—of your Will is probably much less clear, for often it functions subconsciously and if it fails to work or works badly, you instantly tend to excuse, rather than to accuse it, because you call it not your "will" but yourself or "I".

And "I" is the dearest of all created things to you. Do not repudiate this truth, saying that you are not so selfish and self-regarding as all that. It is one of the laws of life, and even sainthood works to that rule, however self-sacrificing the saint may strive to be.

Also do not confuse this will, the governor, with its (i.e. your) servant, the mind. (There is no danger of your confusing it with the body: that, quite plainly, is its mere menial-servant and is constantly obeying with the gladness of a well-trained dog, its master's peremptory, and sometimes exacting, orders.)

The 'I'—your governing will-power—can force the mind into servitude and discipline. Your will can apply your mind to any topic or problem or thing at pleasure. True, the mind sometimes, if not often, breaks away, rebels, and seems ungovernable in its behaviour. But it can be brought to heel again, and the will, by constant practice and exercise of its authority, can break the mind into obedience, like breaking-in an unruly horse. Similarly, the body, too, can be controlled to a truly astonishing degree.

Now no doubt you realise how important and how interesting this psychological truth is. For these reasons, the strength of the will is important. Strengthen your will so that it completely dominates both your mind and your body, and you become a thousand times more effective for every purpose in life. You become a man or a woman in a million. Most folk are the slaves of body or mind, or both. Resolve to make both body and mind your servants.

At bottom, it is chiefly by the strength of your will that your fellows estimate your worth. Few people are truly strong-willed. Few people have *complete* control of their whole selves, though all of course, even the feeblest and flabbiest, attain some measure of control over at least a part of their own selves. Those who are complete masters of themselves, and clearly so, are regarded with a respect bordering on awe by their fellows. They count.

How do you strengthen your will?

It is neither an easy nor a momentary task. Some persons are born strong-willed. But, unlike the achievement of great gifts of body and mind—you cannot make yourself a Goliath in stature or a Mozart in mind if Nature has willed you to be born otherwise, as we have seen in an earlier chapter—you can achieve a strong will. The will, like a physical muscle, grows by exercise. And, again like a physical muscle, it grows flabby and inert by disuse.

Every time your will gains a victory over your body or mind it strengthens itself and its authority. Every time it suffers a defeat by either body or mind it weakens its authority.

Therefore, feed the will with victories and successes. Do not permit it to taste defeats.

To ensure this, take care to set it, especially at first, small and attainable tasks. And exercise it regularly.

Let me illustrate.

Frederick the Great of Prussia, a remarkable King and an equally remarkable man, sensed the all-importance to himself of strengthening his will. As a young man, anxious to study and do more than other men in life, he grudged the time spent in necessary, healthful sleep.

He therefore resolved to do without sleep. To keep awake all night and every night that he might study longer and harder! He resolved to do without sleep over a long period, and with resolute determination set himself so to do.

Alas! strong-willed as the youthful prince Frederick was, he soon found that he had set himself an impossible task. No human will could break the iron law that the human animal must have sleep to live. He tried not to sleep. He fought the tendency to sleep by every means he could devise, by every means in his power.

Useless! He slept.

Inevitably, for Nature forces the living animal to sleep sooner or later. You may do without sleep for a night, for two nights, perhaps even for three. It may be doubted whether there is a single person amongst the toiling millions of London who could keep himself awake for four days and nights. (There are thousands who will tell you that they haven't "slept a wink for a week or a fortnight", but you would be deceived, as they are, if you believed them. For if it were true, they would not be alive to tell the tale.) Soldiers have slept on the march or on horseback: the tortured on the rack.

Do not make the mistake of the great Frederick. Let the tasks you set your Will be attainable ones. And by degrees, make them harder.

And do not give up in despair because of failures. Persist. One of the rewards is, besides the all-important control over mind and body in a thousand ways, the enhanced self-respect, the deep inner self-satisfaction that these mental victories, these Waterloos and Trafalgars and Blenheims, of the will give you.

If you asked me whether I would have a strong healthy body, an active, intelligent, powerful, exceptional mind, or unconquerable will, I should say the last. The first two are bounteous gifts, but without the third they may lead to frustration and futility in life. Many broken-down bodies and many mediocre minds have achieved fame, fortune, and happiness because the will, working out its way, has made the best of them and forced them to its goal.

Put, then, the Will first.

3. The Body

Now for the body. Body-capital is of great importance. People who have brains are seriously apt to underrate it or some part of it. A grievous mistake, as indeed it is to underrate any part of your personality.

Few people look at their body-capital realistically. Its main qualities lie in appearance and health. Though the second is of the greater importance, do not let that blind you to the not inconsiderable importance of the former.

Women, especially younger women, are not in such danger of ignoring the importance of their physical body as men are. They know well the inestimable value of a pretty face, a pleasing expression, a good figure, attractive hands and feet. Also they appreciate the value of these not only to themselves but to others. They know that these are assets and advantages.

The youngest, silliest, and most flighty girl often has more sense on this particular point than many clever men. Nature and her own innate instincts teach her this wisdom. She may be vain and foolish in other things—but not in the emphasis she puts on her face, complexion, teeth, hair, nails, figure, dress, and the rest.

For the truth is the world judges by appearance. Appeal to its eyes and you gain its heart. And once the heart is gained, the mind goes with it.

Appearance, then, is a genuine part of personal body-capital. If you are born good-looking in face and with an attractive figure, exploit it. If you have neither, make the best of what you have. Improve your personal appearance so far as you may.

Everyone knows that a girl with an ugly face and a squat ungainly figure is handicapped in life. The History of Womanhood is strewn with examples of girls and women, starting life poor and friendless and making their way to power and fortune with nothing but their beauty to help them. This is common knowledge. But what is not so well realised is that often men have done the same thing.

The great John Churchill, Duke of Marlborough, the ancestor of the present-day Winston Churchill, got his first advancement in life through his youthful good looks. He attracted the attention and affection of Barbara, Duchess of Cleveland, who gave him his first £5,000. That shrewd youth, Master Jack Churchill, invested it to bring in an annuity of £500 a year and the famous old man, the Duke of Marlborough, aged 70, was still drawing that annuity—and benefiting as he did to the day of his death from his once youthful good looks, and having prudently capitalised them.

B

Not every handsome young man can (or wants to) exploit his face and figure like that. But he can still reap advantages, some direct, some indirect, for people tend to be prejudiced in favour of attractive-looking men quite as much as in favour of pretty women.

Nature may, perhaps, not have been over-kind to you in the matter of facial looks and physical appearance. Then remedy Nature so far as you may. Make the best of yourself. Be well groomed. Be clean and neat. Dress well. Take pains to be well turned-out in every way.

Do not be in the least discouraged if you are of insignificant appearance. Napoleon was of dwarfish stature, so was Lloyd George, and King Richard the Third was a hunchback. Men and women, physically insignificant, can always be of real significance in the world, either by mental attainments, success in their calling, or by attractive and pleasing manners. John Wilkes used to boast—with justification, his acquaintances said—that though he was the most hideously ugly man in Britain, no woman could resist his blandishments and would prefer him to any handsome man if he got the chance of ten minutes' previous conversation with her.

But more important than your appearance is your health and strength. If you have the misfortune to be born sickly and weak that indeed is a heavy handicap in life. A good constitution and a strong frame are incredible advantages—especially to those who know how to preserve them in the temptations of life. The misfortune is that young people never realise the importance of health. They accept it, enjoy it, and too often squander it senselessly.

That is natural. We rarely value what we get for nothing. Healthy youth takes health for granted. Knowing nothing of pain and sickness at first hand, it does not imaginatively realise them. When our eyes, teeth, and stomach function to perfection, we are not in the least sensible of them, nor grateful to them. We just remain unconscious of their very existence.

But get a tiny speck of dust in your eye. Or a toothache. Or griping colicky pains in the stomach. Instantly the afflicted part becomes of paramount importance, and the object, perforce, of its owner's attention, care, solicitude, and interest.

And when men and women, generally in middle-age or later, find that their health, once good or even perfect in youth, begins to go with their teeth, their hair, their eyesight, then—often for the first time—they begin, too late, to take an interest in their health.

But this is trying to lock the stable door after the horse has got out. How strange and sad that most of us only realise the blessing of health when it goes! And health once departed, often, too often, returns no more.

Bodily health and vigour is the basis on which every kind of success in life rests. Then be wise about it betimes. Never risk or injure your health. Give your body its needs: fresh air, good food and drink, sufficient exercise, adequate rest and sleep. Never maltreat your body on any pretext. If you do Nature is unforgiving and duly exacts a penalty.

That sensible man, Dr. Samuel Johnson, used to say: "Sir, I mind my belly. The man who will not mind his belly never minds anything".

Vulgar, no doubt. But sound sense all the same. It is probable indeed that Johnson over-minded his belly by eating and drinking too much—the common fault of his time. This is a fault in the opposite direction, and as common, perhaps more common, than the other.

So neither eat nor drink to excess. Alcohol, we all know, is easily over-done, especially in these drinking days when it is the commonest form of hospitality. Be on your guard against it. But do not fall into the subtler temptation of over-much more respectable stimulants like tea and coffee. These have their insidious dangers. Coffee-drinking to excess is believed to have killed the great Balzac. Many men and women of to-day have ruined their digestion by too strong or too frequent indulgence in "a nice cupper tea".

The natural drink of all animals—and man is an animal—is pure, clear water at ordinary temperature. Even the iced water beloved of Americans—indeed, all over-hot or over-cold foods and drinks—can be dangerous to teeth and digestion, immoderately indulged in. Tobacco, of course, is another habit better unformed, or, if formed, indulged in with strict moderation.

My counsel is to use all these adjuncts to living, alcohol, tobacco, tea, coffee, luxurious food, in strict moderation. If you find you slip into excess, give up any one of them that betrays you.

Here indeed is one of the finest exercises for strengthening your will-power, because its victories in these fields benefit your body as well as your mind.

Another point about health is important. Your health is a great factor in your happiness. The healthy person is the happy person, as a general rule. Any doctor will pick out a dyspeptic man by his miserable facial expression.

Indeed, the close connection between health of body and happiness and health of mind, is now known but not completely understood. For example, modern medicine realises that there is some real relationship between worry and high nervous tension on the one hand and duodenal ulcer and other internal diseases on the other. So, for the sake of their mind, those intellectuals who are apt to despise or neglect the body ought to take care of it.

Compare the influence which unpleasant circumstances or events have upon us when we are well and able to cope with them, with the effect they have when we are troubled with ill-health and depressed. With health, almost everything can give pleasure. Without it, hardly anything is enjoyable.

Have you noticed that when two people meet their first question is: "How are you?" And the answer is generally a health answer. Did you ever ask yourself why this is so? It is because people instinctively feel that one's health is the first and most important thing.

Yet people—without thinking—often sacrifice the lifelong pleasure, advantage, and enjoyment of sound health to a variety of lesser good things. For money, advancement, scholarship, reputation, or even for lesser things, proficiency in a game or for fleeting sensual pleasures.

But this, clearly, is the height of folly.

Make up your mind to avoid this cardinal mistake in living. It is not so easy and trouble-free as it sounds.

For instance, take food. Do you even know much about food-quality? Are you even sure that your diet contains all your body needs to keep the engines sweet and sound? Does it have, for instance, all the calories and vitamins you need for the utmost energy you expend? Quantity and quality both should be right, and food should be not only nutritious but pleasurable. And the same considerations apply to drink.

Then take sleep. Do you get sound, sufficient sleep of restorative quality? You can test this by feeling and being bright-eyed and clear, not given to yawning, absolutely fresh and alert and rested within five minutes after rising. If you feel tired, bog-eyed, used-up, with a tendency to yawn during your matin hours, almost certainly you have not slept well the previous night.

Over sleep it is better to be guided by such definite signs as these rather than by your own mere opinion. We easily are self-deceived over wakefulness and sleep. Also it is not only duration but kind of sleep that counts for good.

Learn how to sleep. How? you may say. By experimenting. Does a high or a low pillow suit you best? A soft or a hard bed? Great warmth or moderate warmth? On your right or left side, or on your back?

The things most conducive to sleep at night for

most of us are: physical fatigue, warmth (especially of the extremities), a quiet and tranquil mind, a relaxed body with a stomach neither empty nor over-full functioning regularly, a comfortable bed in a quiet darkened room. Walk five miles in the open air or "swig a couple," and you will certainly sleep after that.

Over-cerebral, like over-stomachic, activity, is inimical to sleep. Therefore slow down the mind before going to bed. Take care of the brain and the stomach, and the probability is that the rest will take care of themselves. Some people "think in bed", but it is a great mistake "to take your problems to bed with you". Worry keeps people awake more surely than anything else.

Worry should never be tolerated. At bed-time, the mind should be emptied of thought and left tranquil. This is not always easy. The undisciplined mind is apt to let a topic worry it as a dog worries a bone or a rat. Switch the mind off the obsessing topic and on to something more restful and less emotion-fatiguing. Put it to something uninteresting and unimportant. Gradually its tension will die, and relaxed, the mind, and following it the body, will sink into somnolence.

Reflect on this medical fact. Rest is more necessary for the body even than food or drink. You can fast much longer than go sleepless.

4. The Mind

Now we come to the most important ingredient of all in your personality, individuality or complete make-up, namely, your mind or interior self, which consists of your intellect and your emotions.

This interior self deserves the closest and most frequent consideration from you. It also deserves education, which really means improving the mind in two ways: knowledge and skill.

Each of us lives in this little world of his own mind. And this little world of self is far more important to you than the great world without. (Probably you may be tempted to deny this, or at any rate to say "I hope not"—but wait a minute!) For it is this little world, not the great world, that is the principal element in your well-being. The happiness or unhappiness, the satisfaction or dissatisfaction you experience in life, comes not from objective things and circumstances outside yourself, but from the sum total of your ideas, thoughts, sensations, and desires about those things. Indeed, you only apprehend those things and circumstances in your mind.

This is why no external event or circumstance affects two people alike. It is not these things-in-themselves that count; it is their effect upon you, and that depends entirely upon your temperament. To one person a happening is rich, interesting, and significant, meaningful. To another that same happening is dull, poor, tame, boring, and meaningless. Many thousands of Englishmen have led more thrilling and interesting lives than William Shakespeare, the actor-manager, Charles Dickens, the reporter-editor, or Bernard Shaw, the playwright and critic—but how many have had such thrilling and interesting results from their lives to enthral their fellows with?

As everything that happens to, or about, a person

exists only for them in their own consciousness, the most essential thing for all of us is the conditioning of our consciousness. Think of three such men in prison as Cervantes writing *Don Quixote* there, John Bunyan writing *The Pilgrim's Progress* there, and Richard Lovelace writing there his poem, "To Althea from Prison":

> Stone walls do not a prison make,
>   Nor iron bars a cage;
> Minds innocent and quiet take
>   That for a hermitage;
> If I have freedom in my love
>   And in my soul am free,
> Angels alone, that soar above,
>   Enjoy such liberty.

Yes, indeed. These men in prison were never in prison at all. They lived in the spacious realms of themselves. There they were far freer in their jails than many of the bondslaves walking about outside, and probably far more free than their jailors.

But we are all pent within the prison of ourselves. None of us, not the most gifted, can get beyond the limits of his own consciousness, any more than his body can get outside his own skin. The mind imprisons us, and the measure of our happiness is determined by that individuality.

Then how urgent for our good is it so far as we can to educate not only the mind as teachers and schools and universities do, but the whole of that personality in the right direction so far as it will go. A tranquil, cheerful temperament, a flow of genial spirits, a clear, lively penetrating intellect, a realistic yet

B*

imperturbable outlook upon the world and the antics
of one's fellows, a will of one's own—these are great
gifts, and if ungifted by Nature, they are still greater
accomplishments.

Personality, then, is what a man is and has in
himself. It accompanies him when he is alone or in
company, in solitude or in multitude. It is something
none can give but Nature and what none can improve
but himself. It cannot be bestowed or taken away
by his fellows. It is a constant factor amongst the
changes of life, and it comes into play in all circumstances. It is life-long, inimitable, and incalculable.

Certainly though it is decreed by Fate at birth or
before, it is not entirely beyond our power. We can
make the most advantageous use of it. We can strive
after perfecting it. We certainly can develop it by
allowing it full play and by not allowing either
persons, things, events, circumstances, or our own
weaknesses and follies to thwart and frustrate its
working. We can promote and preserve it.

What a man or woman, then, is himself or herself
is what matters most in life. The degree and kind of
one's susceptibility to the environment of persons and
things is everything.

It is a commonplace Latin tag that sums up the
whole of the most desirable personality in the phrase
mens sana in corpore sano (a sound mind in a sound
body). But it cannot be bettered.

And what does this connote? Surely an upright
nature, a capable brain, a joyful or at least an
equable temperament, high spirits, a well-constituted
physique.

But of these diverse gifts, note that the one most conducive to happiness is the flow of genial spirits. An innate cheerfulness or geniality is a great blessing wherewith to face the hazards of life. Fortunately if it be not innate, it can be, and should be, cultivated.

Never lose sight of the fact that you are a body-mind, a psycho-physical organism, each part of which is not separate (as we are too apt to think merely because we separate them in thinking about them), but which are most intimately inter-related. How the mind may affect the body, and the body the mind, is imperfectly understood by either medicine, psychology, or psychiatry, at the present day. But that it does is well known and admitted.

"Neither body nor mind is all important but the ruling part" says Marcus Aurelius. This, as we have seen, is The Will.

Mind-training is of the first importance. An infinite number of books have been written on this subject, stressing the importance of attention, observation, concentration, reasoning, and the like, but interesting as those books are to those interested in the theoretical side of this subject, they are necessarily of little practical value. For the only way to train the mind is to use it persistently on what interests it and on what it is desired to master.

One book of this kind, containing nonsense and good sense in almost equal parts, is the celebrated Annie Besant's *Thought Power*. More down to earth is Ennever's *Your Mind and How To Use It*, and Arnold Bennett's *Mental Efficiency*. Other diverse books are Locke's *Essay Concerning Human Understanding;* Isaac

Watts' *Improvement of the Mind;* Bacon's *Of Studies;*
(Essays Civil and Moral); Gregg's *Use of the Margin;*
and Alexander Bain's *Art of Study* in *Practical Essays.*
Systems for the training of the mind have been
evolved. Doubtless, like algebra and Euclid, they do,
to some extent. But real mind-training is done by use
upon its interests and not upon artificial matter.

Emerson has told us that the hardest task in the
world is to think. It is not. To make thought gene-
rative so that original thought is born, or to make
thought incarnate in action, is more difficult. In a
way, everyone "thinks" and all day long, too, if their
vague, casual, haphazard undisciplined, ineffective
processes of the head can be called "thinking".

What, more perhaps than anything else, leads us
all to effective thought is a thwarted purpose. At
once a problem to solve arises and the mind, roused
to action, secretes thought.

John Stuart Mill analysed "the secret of the
strength and originality of thought" of Jeremy
Bentham, the law-reformer. He described it shortly
as the method of detail. "Bentham," he said,
"treated a whole by separating it into parts; an
abstraction by resolving it in things; classes and
generalities by distinguishing them into the individuals which make them up; and breaking every
question into pieces before attempting to solve it."

Certainly this analytic treatment is of the highest
value in dealing with the problems of living. And how
did Bentham arrive at it? Not by learning it from
books. But by constantly applying his mind to problems that interested him and striving to solve them.

And at the back of that persistent mental application of the mind was, as there must always be, a steady resolute Will, vehemently and consciously directing its servant, the mind to its objective.

We are driven back to where we started. The soul of one's personality is the Will, the directing governing force, which harmonises with the theological and religious dictum of "The Kingdom of God is within you". If, indeed, there is a spark of the divinity within us, as so many have thought, it can be no other than that.

To cherish and preserve one's will both in strength and ardour, is perhaps the most important duty to oneself in life.

Now to put in a short précis the contents of this chapter, these are:

Personality is not the prerogative of exceptional persons, as most people imagine. It is not what you seem to others.

It is what you are. It is what you have in yourself.

Calculate your personal capital. You are a Trinity in Unity, body, mind, and ego (sometimes called the soul, spirit, or the will).

Of the three, the last, the Ego or Will or "I", is the most important. Body and mind are its servants. They can be "broken-in" to obedience.

Strengthen your Ego or Will. It grows strong like a bodily muscle by use and becomes flabby and inert from disuse and lack of exercise.

Important as a strong healthy body, an active, intelligent, powerful, mind are, still more important is an unconquerable Will which makes the best of what body-mind you are.

Put the Will first. Few do.

* * *

As to the body, calculate your physical capital— your looks and health. The importance of personal appearance is better appreciated by women than men. Improve your personal appearance. Manners, dress, mental attainments, can atone for physical insignificance or ugliness.

More important than personal appearance, both to success and happiness, is good health. Never squander health. Preserve it. Life itself will take toll of teeth, eyesight, hair, and strength, however careful you are. Give the body its basic needs: nourishing food, careful drink, fresh air, sufficient exercise and sleep. Moderation in all is the golden rule.

The body reacts on the mind. In theory they can be separated, in the practical business of living they cannot.

* * *

As to the mind—this is the interior world in which you live even more than in the exterior world of other people. Happiness, like the Kingdom of God, is within, not without, you.

You are a prisoner within yourself and can no more get outside your mind than outside your skin. Educate your mind—and not only your mind but your whole trinity-in-unity, your personality.

How to educate the personality? Aim at a tranquil temperament, genial spirits, a clear, lively, penetrating intellect, a realistic outlook and a will of your own.

Personality is a gift susceptible of improvement. Promote, preserve, and perfect it. This is what matters most in life—our real selves, the body-mind or psycho-physical organism that, for good or ill, we are. The way to train one's mind. Useful books.

Persistent application of the mind to what interests it in life is necessary, but behind it all must be the Will, which is a spark of the Divinity.

CHAPTER III

PROPERTY: OR WHAT YOU HAVE

1. Disadvantages and Advantages of Possessions

GREAT possessions are an obvious good. And yet—
so paradoxical is human life, that, as the words
of Jesus Christ to the rich young man show, they can
be no less a hindrance than a help. This is quite as
true in worldly and personal affairs as in spiritual
things.

For, in possessing, you are yourself possessed. You
can perceive this easiest in personal relations, perhaps. A man says "*My* wife and children" but
equally so he is *their* husband and father, with special
disabilities and responsibilities attached to that
status, accordingly. Though they are his, he is also
theirs. Equally is this true of material objects. Possess
a library of books and you, not the books, must
provide shelving, dusting, and accommodation.
Possess a house, and yours are the nuisance and
expense of rates and taxes, repairs, and all the rest.
Possessions, however rich or rare, may be in some
directions almost as disadvantageous as advantageous
to their owner.

This is an aspect of ownership which should never
be ignored. Never own anything that causes you
more trouble (in which is included vexation of spirit,

time which is life, and money) than it is worth.
Remember that "Care keeps his watch in every rich
man's eye".

Probably you say: "I have no great possessions.
Nor am I likely ever to have them." True, great
possessions are an exception, not the rule. But what
is true of great possessions is true (sometimes, however, to a less extent) of lesser possessions. A house-
wife may be every bit as careful and troubled about
her house, which is really the landlord's, as if it were
her own and had her life's capital sunk in its
purchase.

This warns us, above all, never to collect rubbish.
Many people buy things because they are "cheap".
Or because they "may come in useful one day".
Never buy, or even possess as a gift, what is neither
(a) useful, nor (b) beautiful, nor (c) rare, nor (d) of
sentimental value to yourself. Possessions which do
not fall under one or other or all of these categories
tend to become nuisances or afflictions. Scrap them,
or sell them, ruthlessly.

Realise, however, the difference between what may
be called trifling *bric-a-brac* and true *objets d'art*,
which latter may be properly described as treasures.
These are well worth collection. Genuine antiques,
of a fine and rare character keep, and often increase
in value, and so pay for their acquisition, apart from
the pleasure of having them. Sham or spurious or
trifling stuff of this kind is not worth harbouring. It
is far more trouble than it is worth.

It is a good rule in life to buy only the best for
permanent possession.

Against this rule, people say: "But I cannot afford the best." The truth is we can afford nothing else. The best is not always or necessarily the most expensive. And the cheaper is often the dearer in the long run. But if you really cannot get the best (the true best, not what is merely advertised or said to be such) get at least what is servicable and fit for its purpose. Avoid the pretentious, the shoddy, and the second-rate.

Avoiding the second-rate does not necessarily mean avoiding the second-hand. Remember that a diamond which is second-hand differs not a whit from a so-called new diamond.

Spend not only money on possessions but thought upon them. Use care in selecting. Employ your eyes and tongue before buying. Show discrimination. Then you will not go far wrong.

With these advance warnings, remember it is a man's duty in life to himself to acquire and to accumulate all he legitimately and honestly can. Property, or what a man has, is second only in importance to personality, or what a man is.

Reflect on basic facts. You come into the world with nothing. You leave the world with nothing. The Anglican Church Burial Service tells you this in majestic language, and these basic facts you should know for yourself.

But though you begin naked and destitute and end naked and destitute, during the interval between your coming and going, you need a vast quantity of complicated things for your survival, comfort and continuance, not to speak of your happiness and credit in this strange world in which you are, perforce, a sojourner.

Directly you are born, your needs begin. Helpless and useless and vulnerable as the just-born babe is, he or she at once requires skilled attention, Nature's food and drink, shelter, clothing, safety, and continual devoted service. These do not drop from the skies. And to the very moment of your death—and even until you are safely buried in the earth or cremated, thus being finally disposed of—you require an infinitude of ministering accessory things.

If, in your early life, you could see gathered together in one heap, all the life-long food and drink you would consume, all the life-long clothes you would wear, all the money you would spend, you would undoubtedly be startled. What a consumer each of us is! Even the poorest and least-demanding of us.

All of that vast necessitous store has to be got somehow before it is consumed. To the mere maintenance of your life and comfort most of it is essential.

How vital, then, is it that you should have property, using that word in its widest and most comprehensive sense.

2. The Inheritors

And the property obtained—how? Starting with nothing but the Self (which, however, as we have seen, is of transcendent importance) how do we acquire?

Well, if we are lucky, circumstances may aid us. We may be born, as the saying is, "with a silver spoon in our mouths". That is to say, with wealthy relatives or connections from whom we inherit wealth, rank, or other advantages.

This is excellent. It may even be super-excellent if we have the good sense to make the best possible use of our inheritance and treat it, not as something to be wasted and lost, but as a bulwark against the evils, misfortunes, and disasters that its owner may encounter in life. It may even be a disastrous disadvantage, if the heir thinks that the inheritance of wealth is something to be extravagantly dissipated in follies and pleasures, while its owner is absolved from the necessity either of safeguarding it or replacing it through earning any living at all.

To a man of any sense at all, an inheritance is great good fortune which will be prudently husbanded and used. Best of all is it, if the gift is enough to allow him to live in decency and comfort.

He is indeed Fortune's favourite. He is exempt from that poverty and penury which plague his fellows. He is freed from forced labour. He is master of his time and powers. He can pursue a line of life such as disinterested science, music, art or literature or philanthropy, not demanding any sacrifice to money-making. He is exempt from the basic needs such as the necessity to earn by effort his food, drink, clothing, and shelter. He is one in ten thousand, it may be one in a hundred thousand.

He, alone, can say fully, "My life is my own." For it belongs to no employer and no forced labour.

There is a tendency to-day to speak with contempt of those who inherit. It is envious and unjustified.

Such are to be congratulated and to be urged to make the most of their advantage. They are only to be regarded as contemptible if they trifle and idle and waste their inheritance.

To be independent of working for a livelihood and to have, therefore, all the leisure of life, is a condition of which perhaps few men or women are worthy. But, like so many other advantages, such as personal good looks or stature, it has no connection with merit or desert. This is why so many people reprobate it. It outrages their secret ideas of justice. It arouses the secret springs of envy.

But the real world is not a just world. Nature and circumstances laugh at the ideas of human justice and equity. They are not governed by these chimeras of mankind as social communities rightly seek to be governed.

Few—and still fewer, the tendency of social legislation being what it is—inherit. The vast majority of us, including most of the rich, have to work, and work hard, to satisfy our basic needs and desires.

3. What Your Needs Are

What are these needs of yours from birth to death at which hitherto we have barely glanced?

It is your interest to know them exactly. It is your interest to face up to them. For it is you, and you alone, if you are one of the non-inheriting-a-fortune majority, who have to obtain the wherewithal to satisfy them.

First: there are basic needs which you share with

all mankind. Natural imperative needs, which, if unsatisfied, produce physical and irremediable disaster. The physical needs for food, clothing, shelter, warmth, and the like.

Second: there is a lesser and less imperative order of natural needs, both physical and mental, which can be controlled or abstained from, but which are better gratified in moderation. The instinct for love and reproduction, the desire for friendship and fellowship.

Third: there are the comforts, luxuries, and superfluities of life, which moralists say are neither natural nor necessary. But nobody (except the moralist on paper) is going to accept that. "Give me the luxuries of life and I will dispense with the necessities" said a wit. He said well and sensibly.

All of these three classes—in greater or less degree—every man and woman wants. One may even say, cannot do without—though purists may boggle at the last class.

The question in each class for each of us is: How much?

It is impossible to lay down any general rule. It depends so entirely on oneself. One needs luxury to the extent of prodigality (or thinks he does) and also the highest degree of show and splendour that modern conditions in Britain afford. So be it—for him. Another cares little for such superfluities and appurtenances; modest comfort is enough for his peace of mind and body. Indeed, the latter person may feel oppressed and dismayed by what the former would revel and delight in.

Between these two extremes of prodigality and austerity lie nearly all of us, wanting luxury in this field, caring nothing for abstinence in that; and so on.

There is, indeed, no possibility of defining precisely the limits of property (using the word to include all forms of wealth and possession) which will satisfy mankind in general, and certainly not even any man or woman in particular. The amount is relative. It depends upon a person and his own appetites. Each person here has an "horizon" of his own, vague as it may be. About what is beyond his horizon of property for himself he does not care.

So, the dustman does not mourn that he has no diamond studs in his shirt when he goes out to collect refuse. It simply does not occur to him to think of them. These are beyond his horizon—and it is well for him that it is so. Equally, the charwoman washing the doorsteps does not miss the pearl necklace that her circumstances deprive her of. That is beyond her horizon. She is quite content, and indeed happy, with imitation bought at a chain store as a present for her by husband or son or daughter—and it is well for her that this is so.

Conversely, the millionaire or millionairess, unable to have something on which his or her hopes have been set and which perhaps cannot be bought with money, is not consoled by his or her vast wealth for the lack of that one thing.

Such is one of the vagaries of human nature.

You, like everyone else, have an "horizon" of this kind. It is a movable horizon. It is for you to decide what it shall be. But remember this: only discontent and unhappiness comes from making your claims and desires to possess greater than you can possibly get.

Some people suffer much from a continual endeavour on their own part to increase their claims upon the material possessions of this world, while they are powerless, or too indolent, to increase the gains that alone will satisfy their claims. This is a wretched, yet common, condition indeed.

A little straight and clear thinking will keep you from this mistake. Your aim should be the possible and the attainable, not the hopelessly unattainable. Aim at what you can achieve. Let your reach not exceed your possible grasp.

Above all, do not fail to appreciate—what so many do—that your needs in life differ as life goes on. Youth can stand, and even enjoy, hardships which would distress and even destroy the aged. A child needs a nurse; a young man a sweetheart; an adult man a wife and children; an old man a nurse again. The babe lies helpless in its cradle: the man may roam the world and do much in the years of health and strength; but the old man may lie on a couch, bedridden and helpless, needing as much attention and care as in babyhood.

The wheel comes full circle. Remember this great inexorable truth. For it has a bearing on your behaviour.

Your babyhood was provided for by others. You possibly have provided for others' infancies. But, in spite of the Welfare State, you will have to provide for your own old age, just as much as for your daily sustenance as an earning man or woman.

Besides old age, you have to provide for sickness, accident, and the like. No doubt you will say in these modern days that State provision in the form of National Insurance and Old Age Pensions, attends to that.

To a very slight degree it does—to-day! Who can say that it will to-morrow? Or to what degree to-morrow? There is only one safe rule in these matters. It is: Rely on yourself. Make provision for yourself. If your own provision proves to be supplemental to State provision, so much the better.

Making ample provision for one's own personal needs (which may include provision for others, such as those to whom we are bound by ties of blood or affection) is a great part of the art of life. It needs more planning than most people give to it.

First make up your mind what your needs, giving a most generous interpretation to them, are. Then make up your mind to make your gains such that they will cover these until the end of life. Learn the often-repeated lesson of Charles Dickens' Mr. Micawber: "Annual income twenty pounds, annual expenditure nineteen nineteen six, result happiness. Annual income twenty pounds, annual expenditure twenty pounds ought and six, result misery."

That lesson was taught to Charles Dickens by his own childhood sufferings under the improvidence of his own father (Micawber) which put him to toil in a blacking-factory and put his father into the Marshalsea Prison for debt. In those few words you have a great man summing-up a bitter and tragic life-experience for the good of others. Dickens himself in his own later life never forgot that lesson.

All this brings us to the question of that phase of possessing property which is summed up in the magic word: Money.

4. Money and Money's-worth

Money is a unique thing. It has a bad name, even an odious one in theory, but in practice how it is worshipped. The love of money, you are told, is the root of all evil. It may be. But it is also the root of much good.

More humbug is talked of this strange invention of mankind than perhaps of any other, except love. But in truth, no servant of man is more serviceable, for money is prepared to change itself into whatever object our manifold, restless, and wandering wishes hit upon. People will tell you there are things that money cannot buy. Perfectly true; but there are innumerable things that money can buy.

Regard money at its true value. That value is very great indeed. To have sufficient for your whole life should be one of your main aims in thought and activity. For by its aid you can redeem yourself from the slavery imposed by circumstances and your fellow-men; you can attain what Robert Burns, the Scottish poet who knew the disabilities of poverty only too well, called "the glorious privilege of being independent".

When you reflect, too, upon the good things of this life—I do not speak here of a life-to-come— reflect that most good things can only satisfy *one* appetite or one necessity. Thus, food can only satisfy hunger, drink thirst, sleep fatigue, and so on. But money can satisfy many appetites and many needs by its vast enabling powers over the rest of mankind. It can, and will procure an infinite number of good things, and not only material things either, but such things as leisure, service, consideration, privilege and the like.

When you consider how full of continuous needs your life is, you appreciate how many of those needs, material and immaterial, are met simply and sufficiently by "enough money".

Gain, of course, is not the only goal in life. Far from it. If you hunger and thirst after righteousness, for instance, as you well may, to that goal money is utterly irrelevant, as Christ's teaching plainly shows. Money does not heal the diseased, but it may procure them advantages and ameliorations of great benefit to sickness. So if gain is not the only goal, it is one of the goals of life, and it is to be used in doing good to yourself and others.

Never affect to despise or depreciate money. It is the attitude of a fool or a hypocrite. Sensible folk who know its great utility in life, will not believe in your sincerity if you do.

A proper realisation that money is a tireless friend, ready to work for you, means that you will save and then put your capital out at interest. There is one school of modern political thought which condemns interest (as it condemns rent and profits) but I have observed that warmly-professing adherents of that school of political thought never fail to draw from the

Bank or company shares or co-operative dividend, or elsewhere, the interest to which they are entitled. So do not be misled by what I may call the poetic licence with which some politicians talk. Look to their personal actions rather than to their words.

You need not aim at making yourself as rich as the late John D. Rockefeller, in his lifetime said to be the richest man in the world. There is no great advantage for most of us in stupendous riches as compared with riches. Life at best is short, and it is not worth while to spend it in accumulating very much more than your life-needs at the sacrifice of more worth-while activities.

After all, a man has only one mouth of his own to feed, one stomach to fill, one back to clothe, and so on. We are finite and limited beings.

What, then, is the ideal amount of money to aim at?

Surely enough capital to enable a man to live in such comfort, and even luxury, as suits his individual self throughout the rest of his life without forced labour. This sounds reasonable and modest enough. But in a modern civilised community such as Britain, the astronomical extravagance of Governments of all political complexions makes it difficult, indeed very difficult, for the average citizen to accomplish.

And yet many citizens do accomplish it. How? By abstinence from habitual waste, by pension-schemes, insurance-schemes, side-activities, and many other ways. It can be done by resolution, vigilance, and strenuous endeavour. Many British citizens prove that by their success in life along these lines every day.

You, too, can do it. You should do it. The reward is great. Freedom, independence, peace of mind, are prizes beyond "the glittering prizes" of Lord Birkenhead which financial success can gain for you amongst others.

Of purely worldly aims, this financial independence should be the first. Paradoxically, money enables you to be independent of money—you need no longer sacrifice greater and worthier aims to the base need of earning mere livelihood.

In this pursuit, the world being what the world is— a milieu which regards itself as owing the individual nothing that he cannot extort from it—you will need all your persistence, resolution, and will-power. Make no error about that. The saying of Charles Dickens applies: "Ride on. Rough-shod if must be, smooth-shod if may be—but ride on!" This is the only spirit in which you can conquer.

One or two characteristics of your money, often forgotten, should be remembered. Money melts—if not watched. Contrary to the belief of the inexperienced in money-matters, money is harder to keep even than to make. It tempts you to risk itself in a score of ways on the specious excuse of easy increase: as by speculation, gambling, lending, and the like. Be wary, and steadfastly resist such common temptations. Far more money, upon the whole, is lost by such activities than is gained by them.

Why imagine that You—of all the myriads—are selected by Fortune to gain where the majority lose?

This is the fool's bait with which Fortune gulls all
the others. Better be satisfied with the modest safe
increase and remember the adage about one bird
in the hand being better than two in the bush.
Remember, too, the dog that dropped his real bone
in the water beguiled to open its mouth by the sight of
the bigger reflection-bone on the surface of the stream.

Large extravagances are such obvious folly that
few people are in any danger of these. No: what is so
dangerous to you is the habitual small extravagances,
each so small that, despising them as trifling, you
think them of no consequence. Often these add up—
most people *never* add them up—to a dismaying and
staggering total. A daily round of drink, or even a
daily packet of cigarettes, in a lifetime, costs a lot,
for instance. Therefore, before adopting a habit,
calculate its total cost and then consider whether
you can afford that total cost.

I am not advocating you should deprive yourself
of every small self-indulgence that sweetens "the
daily round, the common task". Nor am I urging
avarice and miserliness upon you—though if you
must err, it is better to err on that side than upon the
side of prodigality, extravagance, and wanton waste.
Many a sincere man or woman who would be indig-
nant if you accused him or her of these sins against
self and the community, are guilty of them, not at
one fell swoop, but little by little. They are like the
small persistent drinker who never gets visibly intoxi-
cated, but who kills himself by chronic, if un-
perceived, alcoholism—a sad but common case.

Money may melt in yet another way. Those who

have lived through two great wars do not need reminding of currency devaluation, or of how up to 1914 they handed good gold to their banks to receive back thereafter much-less-worth paper which bought much less, and which continued to depreciate slowly but surely. This aspect of keeping money as money instead of investing it in money's worth, is worth attention, especially by the up-and-coming generation, who, devoid of the rueful money-experiences of war-time, will be apt to overlook it.

Skill in money-handling is not to be despised. Like most skills, it is native to few of us. Like most skills, it has to be acquired by practice.

Now anyone who desires to acquire skill—a violinist, a dancer, a painter, a writer—knows well that daily regular unremitting practice of the art is necessary. Curiously enough, many people will not even look at, or study, the art of safeguarding and increasing their money. Daily attention may be carrying the occupation too far. But once a week, surely, is not too often (for the man who takes his money seriously—as all of us should) to sit down and spend, according to the size and need, a quarter of an hour, a half-hour, an hour, or more, in balancing things up, in consideration of his personal budget. For personal budgets are quite as important to the individual as the Chancellor of the Exchequer's budget is to the nation.

Famous men, renowned for their strong native common sense, have always realised the super-importance of money to the individual. They have never subscribed to the current cant of their day and generation about it. Three such men of differing ages were the great Dean Swift, the famous American Benjamin Franklin, and to come near to our own time, George Bernard Shaw.

Each of them expressed himself on this subject in no uncertain terms. And who would deny that these were men of spirit and of sense?

Writing to his Vanessa, the Dean bade her: "Remember that riches are nine points in ten of all that is good in life. And health is the tenth."

And here are some of the acute sayings on this subject of Poor Richard by Benjamin Franklin:

"Light purse, heavy heart."

"Save—and have. Spend—and crave."

"Three faithful friends: an old wife, an old dog and ready money."

"To be wealthy, think more of saving than of getting."

"Beware of little expenses: a small leak will sink a great ship."

"Get what you can, and what you have, hold. 'Tis one stone that will turn all your lead into gold."

"If you would know the value of money, go and try to borrow some."

Finally, Bernard Shaw, one of the best minds of his generation who began poor and died rich, wrote the following upon "Money".

"Nobody is anybody without money."

"Money is power, security, freedom."

"The only real aristocracy in the world is the aristocracy of money."

"Money is the most important thing in the world. It represents health, strength, honour, generosity, and beauty as undeniably as the want of it represents sickness, weakness, disgrace, meanness, and ugliness."

In this last passage, a great writer is saying not what he was taught to say—people's teaching upon money in his day was very different—but what he has learned by hard experience in suffering poverty in his own person in the school of life.

Can you doubt then what the moral for You is? No doubt Shakespeare's Iago was a great villain. But his advice, "Put money in thy purse", is good advice and you may well remember it throughout life to your advantage. Acquire and accumulate is no bad slogan for young men and young women at the outset of their earning career.

Let us now epitomise the leading ideas of this chapter:

1. Possessions are second in importance to personality. What you possess also possesses you. Collect "treasures" not "rubbish": get the best of its kind.

2. Starting with nothing at birth, you become a bundle of needs from birth to death.

3. Those needs are threefold: (*a*) basic, such as food, drink, sleep, clothing; (*b*) less imperative, such as instinct-satisfaction, physical and mental; and (*c*) the rest, such as comforts, luxuries, and other satisfactions.

4. Find out your own needs and provide for these.

5. This involves money and the study of money.

c

Aim at financial freedom and independence. Gain is one of the necessary goals of life.

6.   Therefore—acquire and accumulate. This is a duty to those dependent upon you as well as to your own future.

CHAPTER IV

LIVELIHOOD AND LEISURE

1. The Choice of a Living

UNLESS you are one of the very few favoured by the gods with an inheritance or a bequest, or have the exceptional good fortune of having your living provided for you by birth—a rare thing nowadays— you will be forced to seek a means of livelihood.

Now livelihood is not life.

Many people make the mistake of thinking that it is. In consequence they sacrifice their life to their livelihood. Some, indeed, make such an utter sacrifice that, apart from their working careers, they can scarcely be said to have any life at all. This is a disastrous error. Life is too precious to be so sacrificed.

That a person's livelihood is of fundamental importance must be conceded. Nevertheless, you yourself, your personality, and your life, are infinitely more important than your livelihood. Even an exigent employer, unless a most unenlightened one, recognises that fundamental fact. How much more important, then, that you should recognise it.

As regards choice of livelihood, the imperative and burning question of course is: "How shall you choose so as to choose what is best for yourself?"

Choice, it is said, is a fine thing. It is also a highly diverse thing. Happily we do not all think and feel alike, and for this reason we do not choose alike. For instance, we do not all say at the outset of our earning career (as we might if men were governed by self-interest alone): "What is the easiest and most lucrative of occupations? Let us all choose that."

Choice, in this particular regard, is not illimitable and unconditional. Various factors, some intensely personal, come into play, and these circumscribe more or less severely each man's or woman's area of choice.

First opportunity. A youth may desire to become an Ambassador of the Crown most ardently. But if he has nothing but a council-school elementary-school education, and has not been to Eton and Oxford or Harrow and Cambridge, or some such equivalent, he will find it virtually impossible to get even one foot on the lowest rung of the diplomatic ladder leading to ambassadorial status. In Gray's country churchyard, there doubtless were mute inglorious Miltons and Cromwells guiltless of their country's blood—merely from lack of opportunity. There are also these possible Miltons and Cromwells in town and village to-day—confined and circumscribed, however, to obscurity and insignificance. "Equality of opportunity"—that canting phrase of the politicians—does not really exist in life at all. A little close thinking applied to the contemporary social phenomena of this wicked world about you, will show you this quite clearly.

All the same, very fine opportunities of all kinds

exist for any and all of us, even the lowliest in the modern world of our era. You hardly need an assurance from me that boys with no more than poverty and a State elementary-school education may become leaders at the Bar or judges on the Bench, famous physicians or surgeons, commanders of armies, renowned men in finance, commerce, or industry, high ecclesiastics, and the like. Similarly with girls starting life as shop-assistants, domestic servants, or in other humble and even menial occupations. These may become, like the late Margaret Bondfield (whom I knew personally) a Cabinet Minister. Miss Bondfield owed her elevation to nothing more than sound common-sense backed by a strong will and a clear idea of whatever she wanted. Hosts of girls "starting from scratch" with nothing but themselves, have made brilliant marriages or become nationally, or internationally, famous women.

Such successful persons took advantage of such opportunities in life as presented themselves.

Look well, then, to the opportunities ready to your hand. Do not despise them, if small. Do not spend time sighing after greater ones. Rather grasp the nearest and best to hand.

For instance, if there is a family business, however humble, in the offing, do not superciliously and snobbishly think yourself too good for that, as many young persons of some education are apt to do. Instead, coolly estimate its present, and its probable future, prospects and worth. Are you so sure you can do better, or so much better, launching out to swim on your own and wastefully jettisoning this life-belt to begin with?

Or by "following in father's footsteps", there may be an initial impetus of great value. Your father may be favourably known in the trade, profession, or occupation that he follows. Or your family may. This may provide you with a flying start, and give you a chance denied to your competitors.

So much for opportunity in the decision as to what you should do for your livelihood. The great Italian Machiavelli, tutor of princes and kings, who knew more of life, human-nature, and polity than most men, has some pregnant verses on "Opportunity" which you should read.

The next factor after opportunity is predilection. A great question is what would you like to do as your life-work? This is of vital importance, since so much of your lifetime and your self will be devoted to your work, that you should choose work that is congenial.

Work that one hates, or even dislikes, becomes a soulless drudgery that one does not do well. In what you dislike, you are very unlikely to shine or excel. What you like best you may very well do best—though this rule is not absolute and has exceptions to it.

But what you like best, the calling you wish to pursue, may be impractical. For instance, if you are a stage—or film—struck girl destitute both of good looks and acting ability, or a youth who wants to paint and cannot. Then, in such cases, the aspirant may have either to choose again and choose something different, or compromise by choosing the next best thing (as where the mediocre painter becomes the good art-critic, like John Ruskin, for example).

Personal predilections are of real moment here. They are not to be over-ruled lightly, as they may perhaps be in many other fields. This fact is, fortunately, widely recognised by those caring for the young, nowadays.

But your tastes are not everything. Your talents (or their absence) are also a highly relevant factor. Very often the youthful beginner is fascinated by a way of life for which he has no real aptitude. Certain professions, such as the stage for girls and the Bar for boys, have an especial glamour. They dazzle. As the candle-flame attracts the winged tribe, so these avocations attract a romantic tribe of boys and girls—sometimes as disastrously. Later they may find a truer, if more humdrum, *métier*.

There are certain occupations in which any average person of fair intelligence and ordinary perseverance may succeed to a respectable degree. Such livelihoods do not demand very specialised aptitude or gift beyond those possessed by the majority. Often these are safe and sound, and though commonplace in themselves, are worthy enough for those of quiet, sensible temperament and mediocre ambitions. The clerk, who may or may not become a manager, the civil servant who may or may not rise to the higher grades in Government service, the teacher who may or may not attain the headship of a school, are all instances of this kind. Such occupations may well attract those who are suited to them.

But sometimes he or she who looks for a livelihood, is blessed above all others, in that instead of their choosing a livelihood, a livelihood chooses *them*. In other words, their destined, or pre-destined, calling so powerfully attracts them and they are so obviously fitted for it, that for their individual selves there is no question of anything else. Mozart as an infant could, and did, play the violin and was clearly marked for music from his cradle. Such fortunate persons are called, as many a priest or minister feels himself "called by God", from birth or early life to their destined vocations.

These, however, are the fortunate few. Most of us have to rely upon opportunity, liking, and ability to surmount examinations or the like.

And not all of those who imagine they have a "call" to a certain way of life are right in so thinking. As we have seen, some are tragically self-deceived, partly by vanity, partly by the glamour or romance of the life that appeals to them. In Somerset Maugham's great novel, *Of Human Bondage*, there is a minor female character who exemplifies this. She studies art in Paris and resolutely strives to be a great artist, for which she believes herself fated. But she has no real talent; and after a series of long, pitiful, and self-respect-destroying struggles to win to her much-desired goal, she suddenly realises her mistake and commits suicide in despair. The character is true to life, and very likely was drawn by the author direct from life.

So if you think that you have "one clear call" to one way of livelihood only, unless it be a spiritual vocation with which there is no arguing, take care. Be very sure of the call. Especially be sure if it be a hazardous and uncertain way of livelihood, such as the stage, literature, music, or any vocation calling for inborn talent.

Reflect, too, that most people—and the odds are that you are one of them—could succeed by perseverance and average intelligence in a dozen callings or more. And if you have no special choice, why not choose a calling that is lucrative and congenial?

After the choice is made, perseverance, intelligence, and energy applied to the calling, are paving-stones upon the pathway to success.

2. One Livelihood or More

Most people are capable of one livelihood only. And in most cases it is perhaps wisest for them to concentrate on one only. Especially is this so in the early or prentice stage.

But some men, when they have mastered their profession, trade, or calling, have superabundant energy and great ambition. Having mastered one field, they look for another field to conquer. Or they wish to supplement their income.

A fine example of a resolute man who carried on two livelihoods simultaneously and successfully, was Anthony Trollope, the famous Victorian novelist. He was a distinguished and hard-working Civil Servant in the Post Office. But that was not enough for him.

Being the son of a most remarkable woman, Frances Trollope, who, at 54 (finding herself with a sick and unsuccessful husband and a family of con-

c*

sumptive children and no money) started to write novels before breakfast daily. In the next twenty-six years this amazing wife and mother produced 114 readable and saleable books that kept the Trollope family in decency and comfort. Mrs. Trollope was one of the too-little-appreciated heroines of English life.

Anthony could not forget that example. What son, indeed, could? He emulated his mother, and by the same method of early-morning rising and pre-breakfast working. So for three hours daily he was Trollope the novelist: for the rest of the day he was Trollope the Civil Servant.

You may read the admirable story of both mother and son in Trollope's *Autobiography*. Not only is it an inspiration to the striving, it is also a strictly practical showing of the humble, plodding, way to success. Read it both for profit and enjoyment.

What Trollope could do, others can do. Others, in fact, have done it ever since. But let it not be recommended as the only way. Indeed it is not. There is no "only way". For some people it is better to concentrate on one livelihood and attain excellence in that field. There is such a thing, be it remembered, as falling between two stools.

And yet—how many famous men and women have followed more than one path of livelihood! The present Prime Minister of England, Sir Winston Churchill, is a notable example. In his youth he was both soldier and journalist: in later life, politician, author, historian, and artist. It is not given to many to be so versatile and so successful.

In modern England, too, the high rate of taxation and its incidence, are both powerful disincentives to extra effort. So great a proportion of our earnings do the Government and the local authorities and the national service-monopolies take from us that many people feel, at the date of writing this, that the extra effort is not worth while. But it should not be forgotten that money-reward is not the only reward of work. There is the personal acquisition of greater skill. There is increased reputation. There is also the pleasure that arises from self activity to one's fullest powers.

You, and you alone, can decide whether you will put all your earning efforts in one direction, or some in one, and some in another. You, and you alone, can judge whether your energies are fully employed in your daily routine. Or whether you should exceed the daily programme.

But even if you concentrate on one calling with fierce and unremitting intensity, either from love of it or determination to succeed in that field, or in more than that field, beware of allowing livelihood to monopolise your whole life. There must be relaxation in every person's life or efficiency in the highest and broadest sense will suffer.

3. Concerning Leisure

Which brings us to the problem of leisure. Leisure is no less important than livelihood and, in some phases, even more so.

Indeed, it has been said with some truth that what a man does with his leisure when he is alone, is his real religion. In some cases that may well be so. But not in all.

Modern people have plenty of leisure. It may even be that they have too much. Working a five-day week is not enough to exhaust the mental and physical machines of the average man. Nor is a five-and-a-half day week. Leisure, of course, is an indubitable boon. The mischief is that many British folk do not know what to do with their leisure when they have it.

Leisure, indeed, needs as much planning as livelihood. But many folk are so used to having their livelihood time organised for them by "the boss" (whether that boss be a person, a Company, or a way of work) that they are at a loss to organise their leisure. They fritter it away in boredom and folly.

Yet other people turn their leisure into work-time —an equal mistake.

Leisure's true purpose is for relaxation and rest— using those two words in their widest meaning. A change of occupation can be a real relaxation and repose, even though it may involve strenuous muscular or mental activity.

So the sedentary office-clerk may spend a summer evening or a fine week-end working hard in his garden—and feel mentally and physically invigorated by the change of occupation. Or the manual worker may read a difficult book with delight and reward, feeling equally invigorated by that change.

Perhaps the danger of modern leisure is that modern life offers too many varied distractions for its spending. We have radios and television, games and sports of every description, theatres, cinemas, music-halls and concerts, dancing, swimming, walking, reading, and a hundred other activities and hobbies that we may take up. It is no bad idea "to try everything once" in this field of leisure, and see what best suits your tastes, your pocket, and your convenience.

Be enterprising in exploring what to do with your leisure. Most people in this regard are not enterprising enough. They tend to take up the nearest thing or the hobby of their friends. They do not even try other things that might suit their natures better and please them more. Most of them are satisfied to "gape"—at football matches, at stage-shows, television-screens, and the like. But activity is better than passivity, and the acquisition of "skills" is worth much.

Can you drive a car? Can you swim? Can you pilot a plane? Can you ride a horse? Can you row or sail a boat? Can you talk or read a foreign language? How do you know, if you have never tried, whether the acquisition of any one of these personal "skills" might not enhance and enrich the pleasure of your life?

Have you explored England, Scotland, Ireland, or Wales? Or the adjacent islands, such as the Scillies, the Channel Islands, and the Isle of Wight, the Isle of Man, or Lundy Island? If not, why not? How do you know what delights may not be in store for you in some part of any one of these, if you have never been there?

And what of foreign travel? In these modern days of supersonic speed, it is so easy to travel fast and far.

You cavil at the expense? But I know a young London clerk, who, on his junior clerk's wages, managed in the leisure of his week-ends and holidays to travel the whole world within the space of two years and a half.

"I was determined to see the world. And not to spend too much of my small hard-earned wages either on mere fares," he told me. "So I took jobs in aeroplanes, and the Companies helped me. I did it. And what a gorgeous two and a half years I had."

Another youngster, a girl, was equally determined, but her interests lay not so much in seeing the world as in "seeing life" from the angle of sophisticated young womanhood. In one year, confining herself to the West End of London, she got personally acquainted with life at Claridge's, the Ritz, the Berkeley, the Savoy, and knew the world of fashion and the stage so thoroughly that she changed her occupation from a London teashop waitress to the manageress of a large London hotel. This was the fruit of her well-organised leisure.

"And how I enjoyed it," she said to me. Well, she deserved to. She showed initiative, enterprise, and determination. She deserved her reward.

The use of leisure can be foolish or fruitful. Its use is not necessarily wasted because it is not directly purposeful. A man may take his ease with a drink or a smoke, in a restaurant or even a public-house, or at home. This may put no money in his pocket or ideas in his head. Nevertheless, this doing nothing may be all right for him—in moderation. Apparent idleness may not be real idleness. We need to dream as well as to do.

The mischief comes when too much time is wasted on the specious plea of relaxation or rest. Or when leisure is used harmfully in eating or drinking or smoking or gambling to excess, or indulging in trivial frivolities, which do not really amuse or interest the participant. It is quite astonishing how much time one can lose in (for instance) unmeaning and tiresome social conversation with people who are not worth one's while and who tire, disgust, and bore one with their inanities about little nothings and pettifogging gossip.

One needs to be on one's guard against losing one's leisure, as one needs to be on one's guard against losing one's money. It is the easiest thing in the world to be cheated out of one's leisure by one's own thoughtlessness or by one's complaisance towards other people.

Leisure is a valuable asset. It is life-time. See it is not filched from you either by your own follies or the unconscious machinations of the social world surrounding you. It is not an inexhaustible store. Therefore expend it wisely and according to plan. Don't, whatever you do, fling it away to no profit or real pleasure at all.

In short, give as much thought to the organisation and use of your leisure-hours as to your working-hours. This will richly repay you.

Now to sum up the main life-lessons of this chapter:

Never sacrifice too much life to livelihood. In the choice of your livelihood have regard to (1) opportunity; (2) personal predilection. Beware of the merely romantic and the impractical.

If you have no natural vocation, choose a calling that promises to be lucrative and congenial. There are occupations in which anyone by perseverance, energy, and average intelligence, can succeed respectably.

Consider, too, whether one calling or more than one should be aimed at.

As to leisure, employ this profitably in the widest sense of that word. Leisure is life-time, just as livelihood is, and must not be frittered or trifled away in what does not rest, relax, please, or profit, in some way. To lose one's leisure is as disastrous as losing one's money. Thought on its wise and congenial employment will amply repay you.

CHAPTER V

THE ENVIRONMENT OF OTHERS

1. Friends, Enemies and Indifferentists

SELF-SUFFICIENCY is amongst the greatest of felicities. The ancient Greek philospher, Aristotle, knew this when he proclaimed: "To be happy means to be self-sufficient."

Nevertheless, no man can live entirely to himself. Still less, perhaps, can any woman. For women seem intended by their very physical make-up, as well as by their mentality, for relationships with other human beings. But, like it or not, the religious dictum that "we are members of one another" is to some degree true, and we are also, despite the utmost personal independence, dependent upon the community, the aggregate of humanity in which we dwell.

None in modern days can live as a hermit, completely in solitude, or like a Trappist monk, having no communion with his fellows. This being the case, since we must have relations of various kinds with our fellow-men, it behoves us to study how these may be conducted.

Diplomacy and foreign affairs are admittedly of importance in international concerns. They are not less important to individuals. Quite as much skill, quite as much finesse, quite as much circumspection, may be involved in the second as in the first.

Every day and in every way, you are going to encounter your fellow men and women. What will be the result of each and every encounter? That depends, you will say, on many things. For instance, who they are and the nature of the present encounter and past relationships. True. But it depends far more upon yourself.

Get that fact well and firmly into your mind. It depends mostly upon you. Not as you may be tempted to believe, upon "the other fellow"—be that other fellow a man or a woman. You are the master, if you resolutely and secretly choose to have it so in this matter—yes, even the master of your employer or your social superior.

It does not matter who or what the other person is. Your superior, your inferior, your equal in position and intelligence. What does matter is your being able to understand and command the situation arising from your encounter and relationship with him, her, or them.

No light matter to be adequate to, and dominate all, situations, you will agree.

Can you always command the situation? Can that really always be done? It sounds a tall order. But unquestionably it can.

You will be eager to learn how. Well, first you must understand any situation before you can command it. That is obvious.

What is the general situation underlying all such encounters? Just this: Every person you encounter is potentially a friend, an enemy, or an indifferentist. That is true of every one you meet. Some may not fall and fit exactly into one of those clear-cut categories. For instance, John Jones, your stable-companion at work, may be friendly to-day over one matter, indifferent to-morrow over another, and dead hostile over yet another the day after to-morrow. Human relations, it is true, fluctuate like English weather. But, by and large, you know that the categories of enemies, friends, or indifferentists broadly fit all your acquaintances and on all occasions.

Such being the indubitable case, how then? Your clear duty to Yourself is to metamorphose friends into warmer friends, enemies and indifferentists into friends. Perhaps you boggle at the intimate word "friends". Then I will substitute the term "helpers and well-wishers." Or even "aiders and abettors of your advantage".

A powerful friend, rich, prominent, influential, if he desired to help you forward, could do much for you, could he not? He might hand you money or money's-worth, or a responsible post, for example. But any friend is a friend. It is amazing how much good unimportant friends can do, as every politician knows. It is also amazing what evil unimportant enemies—even a single one—can do likewise.

You cannot have too many well-wishers and helpers as you move through the difficulties of life. If you can say, "Everyone of my acquaintance has goodwill for me, speaks well of me, and will neither consciously do, nor say, anything to retard my advantage", you are highly fortunate, as you will agree. Probably (human beings being what you know some of them to be) you do not think that so desirable a consummation as the one I have outlined can be attained.

But it can. Or something so very near it as makes no odds. With care, vigilance, and skill, it can be engineered.

Let me add one word to this. Do not imagine that there is a single exception to the rule that you should turn everyone into friends. There is none so poor, so humble, so unimportant, that you "need not bother" with him. Remember the fable of the mighty lion caught in a strong net of cords and of the humble mouse-friend that nibbled the cords and freed the captive when the lion's strength availed him nothing.

Remember, too, that what the beggar mutters in the alleyways to-day, the King on his throne hears to-morrow, according to an Arabian proverb. There are beggars and kings in your life, although they may be known as office-boys and managing-directors, perhaps.

The rule is absolute: Make friends, that is well-wishers, helpers, sources of goodwill, of everybody. Repeat—as the telegram-girls say—*everybody*.

2. The Way

"But how?" you will ask. Probably you will add: "In many cases what you suggest is quite impossible. No one could make that hateful fellow Robinson into a friend. Or a well-wisher. Certainly I cannot. In the colloquial vulgarism, he 'loathes my very guts'. And

I loathe him. I'd rather not have him as a friend."

But this is not the language of good sense. Still, for the moment let us leave the difficult Robinson out of the discussion. Let us first deal with "How".

How then shall we turn the average person into a friend? The answer to this is "By the art of pleasing". Yes. It is as simple as that.

Study and practise this art. It is not difficult. It does not require residence at a University, skilled lecturers, or the reading of numerous text-books. As the great Lord Chesterfield has pointed out in his *Letters to His Son*, it requires only the wish to please and the resolve to practise being pleasant.

Please others—and they will be pleased with you. The formula, carried into practice, works like a charm. Or, more accurately, perhaps, like a miracle.

On this fascinating subject here is another of Chesterfield's words of wisdom, "I can promise you", he says, "that if you make a man like himself better he will like you very well." Subtle, is it not? And yet how simple to learn. It is well worth learning. Much better worth learning than more pretentious subjects of education on which life-time and money is prodigally spent.

Ah! what trifles please. This woman, a few careless words of compliment on her beauty: that man, a flattering phrase on his brains. It is surprisingly easy. Each of us has a weak and vulnerable spot, and it is not difficult for the keen observer to see and touch it.

Nor is it always what is said that counts. It is very frequently the way it is said, as everybody knows.

You may please or offend a hearer merely by saying "Good morning" to him.

And it is as easy to please as to offend. Also it costs you as little effort, and the one brings profit where the other brings loss. Desire to please, and you will quickly perceive the way. A girl who desires to please her lover does not go to evening-class or pore over books: she follows her instinct. She uses her eyes on his face to see how he responds. A youth who wants to please a girl does not need to go asking his mother and father: he very quickly learns to cope with that situation. By his attentions to the girl he very quickly wins her attention to him—the first step—and he gets as far as that instinctively. By his attentions he gains her attention.

In this connection, you should take yourself very seriously in hand. Politeness and consideration for others pay great dividends in goodwill: they ingratiate you with others quite insensibly. Study to be pleasant, polite, and friendly. Go out of your way even to show regard for others. They will come highly to regard you as a consequence.

If this sort of thing cost money how willingly would we spend it! It costs only the small coins of good manners, compliments, and the like; sometimes even the base counterfeit coins of flattery will do. If people prefer bad money, you are not cheating to give them what they want. The baseness of flattery is not in the flatterer (who knows that good money would not be accepted as such) but in the fool who accepts flattery as his or her due, and as the real thing.

You will, indeed, be astonished, should you practise

compliment, praise, and appreciation, what gross and palpable flattery people accept—especially on their weak point or points. This is the teaching of men of the world, but people of higher morals will not, of course, stoop to such conduct.

And if you feel you do not know what will please any individual, ask yourself: "What pleases me?" It is true that we are not all alike, and that one man's meat may be another man's poison. Yet basically we are very similar. Since you do not like being ignored, insulted, and injured, be very sure others do not. Since you *do* like being noticed, praised, appreciated, and so on, be very sure others like it just as much as you do.

Indeed, the master-key to human-nature is Vanity. Even the least sensitive of us is sensitive to any wounding of his *amour-propre*. Never wound another's personal vanity. He or she will hardly forgive you if you do. People, as they indeed say, cannot bear to be "made to look small", i.e., to be humiliated in the eyes of their fellows. Or even in their own eyes.

Note that it is not only by direct means—large compliments and small gifts as a lover to his sweetheart—that you prevail with others. You also prevail by indirect means. For instance, does it strike you as strange that a good-looking girl gets good-will directly people see her, merely because she is lovely? It is very unjust, no doubt. But people and the world are like that. The pretty girl's face and figure are as good as—or better than—letters of recommendation. At sight of her, others are conquered or half-conquered.

Strange as this is, yet you know very well from your observation and experience that it is true.

But equally true, though in a less degree—and perhaps unrealised by you—a good appearance in a man, due merely, it may be, to careful and tasteful clothing, and a modest erect bearing, helps also. The eye of the beholder is a direct channel to the heart.

Get people's eyes pleased and you gain their hearts. Gain their hearts and you gain their heads. Then you have gained all.

It is no small achievement to gain friends and to influence people in your direction. Make yourself your own Public Relations Officer: destroy enmity by replacing it with friendship; eliminate friction; create confidence, goodwill and help. Incidentally, you will improve your own manners and character as a by-product of your efforts, for you will find it necessary to do to others as they are desired to do unto you. How much more pleasant and profitable communal life and commerce with your fellows will become, I need hardly tell you. You will discover that for yourself in living in this way.

3. Human Liabilities and Human Assets

Not long ago, in a railway carriage, I heard a scrap of conversation that aroused my intense curiosity. I would gladly have heard more.

One elderly man said fretfully to another: "My wife's a terrible liability. And has been ever since the day I married her thirty years ago. It's been absolute hell, my married life."

The other replied: "Yes. Mine was when I first

married her. But she quickly turned herself into an asset, and she's been my finest asset ever since."

"Oh, you could marry anybody and turn her into an asset, Jack—except my old woman," retorted the first. "Not even you could make a go of her."

Looking at the calm, sensible, confident, face of the second man, I could well believe that he could "make a go" of almost any marital partner, however unpromising.

I heard no more. For the train stopped at a station and I had to get out. This intriguing fragment was all I heard.

Turning human-liabilities into human-assets is quite as interesting and rewarding as turning business-liabilities into business-assets. It is only another phase of turning enemies into friends. We are told by the Bible to forgive our enemies, and no doubt this is excellent advice. But the way I put it is "Transform your enemies"—then you will have no difficulty in forgiving them. The doctrine of Reconciliation is not only good religion: it is also good business and good worldly wisdom.

Every friend is an asset; every enemy a liability in life. And it is a terrible state of affairs indeed when one's enemies are one's nearest folk. If a man cannot turn his wife, if a wife cannot turn her husband, into a friend, the marriage is (as John Selden, that cynical and shrewd old Tudor lawyer, said of marriage in general) "a desperate thing". It had better be, as Radical reformers used to say of the House of Lords, mended or ended.

Somerset Maugham, the greatly skilled story-writer, once said that he cannot meet a man or woman for the first time without being able to make a story out of them. That is remarkable. But you should be able to parallel that. You and I should not be able to meet any man or woman without gaining some advantage, something worth while, from the encounter.

Be very sure that if not, the fault is yours, not theirs. For every human being has something of worth in them if you can find it out. It is there. It is there for you if you can only get at it. This is worth remembering. Often the fool or the bore is intelligent and interesting if only the right note is struck.

Looking over an old journal that I once kept, I came upon the following striking entry: "For each of the three days in this week my personal expenditure has been exactly NIL."

This interested me so much that I read back to see if there was an explanation of this singular phenomenon in my ordinary working-life. Usually on food and transport in working-time my personal expenses are necessarily substantial. I found that one friend had called for me with his car each morning; yet another had asked me out to lunch; still another had given me tea; and the first had also brought me back home—a total journey of 200 miles. All this was entirely unsolicited. Incidentally, it saved me much money and a good deal of personal effort such as going by rail would have entailed.

That illustrates something of the value of friends amongst one's associates in business. None of these contributors to my welfare and convenience were intimate personal friends. Nor did any of them look for any return. They were animated solely by good-will.

It might have been very different.

This happy and pleasant state of affairs was not calculated by me. It arose from what might be called by the unthinking, accident rather than from design. Yet it was not an entirely fortuitous combination of circumstances. Indeed, few things are. It arose from goodwill in a number of quarters cultivated over a long period.

The smallest of friends may be valuable. The least of enemies may be deadly indeed. Reflect on this striking fact: the smallest microbic enemy of the human race may be the bacillus of Asiatic cholera. Yet if it gets into your blood-stream it multiplies faster than any other known. Failing its destruction, you will be dead in twenty-four hours.

4. Groups and Groupism

Hitherto we have looked at other people as individuals. But you will encounter them not only as individuals, but as conglomerations into groups, herds, committees, societies, and associations, of all sorts and kinds.

Organisation, and perhaps over-organisation, is the note of our day. You can hardly escape membership of this, that, and the other organisation. Inevitably, and sometimes involuntarily, you are a member of some: a Briton by birth, a member of a Church by infant baptism, a scholar by legal compulsion, and a fighting service unit by compulsion, and so on. But, in addition to these you will be solicited to become a voluntary member, and perhaps an office-bearer, in many more organisations.

Two things you will find are required of you by almost all these groups. One is your money. The other is your time. Two of the most precious things you possess.

A subscription to one organisation may not be a great cost. A brief attendance at one committee may not take much life-time. But a subscription to ten, twenty or thirty good causes and excellent societies is a heavy matter: attendance at a dozen meetings a week, fortnight, or even month, is a good slice out of the year. Clearly you must exercise restraint here.

The number of societies is legion. Many are necessary; most are admirable. A lot of them have objects that appeal not only to your purse but to your heart and mind also. Nevertheless, it is necessary to harden your heart like King Pharaoh and steel your mind against the blandishments of many of them. You must be rigidly selective. Otherwise you will have too little money and time left for personal concerns.

In choosing what groups you will join and support, you need to make a calm appraisal of those which interest you. This is by no means easy. It is also an intensely personal matter, and therefore only very general guidance can be given. You are your own best guide here.

But this may be said. According to modern psychologists, we can all, broadly speaking, be divided into two classes, called introverts and extroverts. An introvert is one who lives chiefly in the inner life of himself or herself, in his or her own private world of thought and feeling. An extrovert is one who lives chiefly in the outer world of things, events, and other people. One is subjective: the other objective. Perhaps more women than men are introverts and more men than women extroverts—though this may be challenged by some.

Anyhow, according to whether you are an introvert or an extrovert, whether you are solitary or gregarious, you will tend to avoid, or to join your fellows, whether for social or organisational purposes. It all depends upon your inborn temperament, though habit and education may modify your natural reactions.

Yet whatever type you belong to, you may usefully ask two questions of any society or organisation before you commit yourself to joining it. One is: what will be required from me in money, time, and the like, through joining it? The other is: what benefits (if any) shall I get out of it? The word "benefits" is used in its widest sense, for even if you unselfishly join a society like one for the prevention of cruelty to children or animals, you get the benefit of advancing a worthy cause and fulfilling your laudable desire to assist good against evil.

These two questions you should always ask. Never join any of these organised bodies from weak surrender to appeals or solicitations. Choose with discrimination amongst the almost infinite number that exist.

Considerable benefits may be gained of an indirect order from joining a society, quite apart from the direct ones advertised. Useful acquaintances may be made, incidentally. Fresh and deeper interests may arise. Like-minded people meet and exchange ideas on a subject of special interest. The results cannot be other than mutually beneficial, and this fact is well-recognised on all hands.

It is a curious fact that any organisation or group is a very different thing from the individuals, or even the total of individuals, composing it. It is an entity, yet an abstract entity at best. Often it attracts loyalties as the State, the Church, the School, the Regiment, the Trade Union, the Club, all do in their several ways. That loyalty in some instances becomes so exaggerated as to become subservience, and real evil and harm may come of that, as we all know.

The golden rule is, in joining any group, either voluntarily or involuntarily, never to sink your individuality entirely in it, but only temporarily at need and for strictly limited objects (as where a civilian becomes a soldier in war-time, for instance), and never to forget that the group, however important (even the State, for instance), exists for you and that you do not exist for the group. This seems obvious. But it is contrary to what many, perhaps most, people tend to practise, if not to preach.

Recapitulating briefly the lessons of this chapter, these are:

1. None can live to himself. Your friends, enemies, and neutrals must be reckoned with. Metamorphose, by taking thought, friends into warmer and truer friends, and others into friends.

2. You cannot afford one enemy—even the least significant.

3. Study the art of pleasing. It requires only the will to do it. The master-key to Human Nature is Vanity.

4. Turn your human-liabilities into human-assets.

5. Study the advantages and disadvantages to yourself of Groupism. Choose these with discrimination.

CHAPTER VI

THE ENVIRONMENT OF PLACE

1. Home

You are a land-animal. That fact confines you to the earth and its atmosphere perforce. But need that fact do what it generally does with most people, confine you for most or all of your life to an almost infinitesimal portion of the earth's surface?

Clearly in these modern days it need not and should not. Since transport has conquered the earth and the air, there is no reason, except your own apathy or lack of cash, why you should not share in that conquest.

Make up your mind that travel in all its forms, especially air travel in spite of its present dangers, is for you. Travel will broaden and deepen your knowledge and experience of life at first-hand.

But before dealing with your world-environment, we must deal with the infinitely smaller, yet even more important, place-environment in which you live the greater part of your life: the spot you recognise as your usual abode, called Home.

Now as an independent self-sufficing entity, you need a home of your own. If you are very young, or if you are married, then it may be impracticable for you to possess an entire home of your very own.

Nevertheless, no human being past childhood ought to be so poor that he, or she, does not possess at least a room of his or her very own. Be it study, or workshop, or attic, or shed, or bedroom, without some such solitude, tolerable life is impossible. However gregarious one may be by nature, this is essential at times if one is to develop one's full life.

A place of one's own—where one can be alone—is essential.

And that place, however small and humble or large and spacious, should be made one's very own in the fullest sense of the phrase. That means not only should it be sacred to one's self, but it should be used as an expression of one's personality. Here the student will have his desk and seat and his shelves of books at the very least, or the mechanically-minded his different table, his tools, his bits and pieces, and so on. It is no small pleasure, bit by bit, to make the room, by well-thought-out additions, more efficient, more comfortable, more native to one's self, until it exactly expresses what one is and what one wants to do there, and reaches the acme of usefulness, beauty, and pleasure for its occupant.

For just as the fish must have its water, and the bird its air, so you and I must have the immediate environment native to us for comfort, pleasure, and harmonious self-development.

Even poverty is no excuse for not turning one's environment, so far as may be, into something suited to oneself. This counsel may prove troublesome in many cases. But it can be done, and should be done.

D

For the reward in peace of mind and satisfaction, is great, apart from the obvious advantages.

Further, it is quite extraordinary what the determined and thoughtful occupant of a room, a flat, or a house, can effect in the way of improvement. Most people are far too willing, however, as they say "to put up with" their surroundings, to their detriment.

But this is a world where nothing that can be changed for the better should be "put up with". For there is a penalty in acquiescing in sordid, squalid, and unsuitable surroundings. They depress the spirits; they affect the mental attitude; they pollute one's outlook, slowly, insensibly, but none the less surely. In Bernard Shaw's phrase, "they drag my life down to planes of vulgarity where I cannot breathe".

Rather than "put up with" your immediate environment, resolve to make that immediate environment put up with you and your native needs.

If the home-environment is altogether antipathetic and beyond tolerance, do not wear yourself out warring fruitlessly against it. Leave it. The world is wide. Strike out on your own and make a home, a true home, for yourself. In certain circumstances that may be the only thing to do.

The point is that your little routine-environment, whatever it be, must be suited to your nature. The gipsy in his caravan, the artisan in his council house, the peer in his ancestral mansion, the bishop in his cathedral-close palace, the foreign royalty visiting Britain in his suite of rooms at Claridge's, the Royal Family in their palace, may be equally well-suited and desire nothing better. Take care, then, that like these, your environment fits you.

Suppose you are in such a position as to be able to choose, within reason, the style of house, and even, within limits, the locality where you will live.

Then do not make the mistake, so many do, of not really exercising the full choice that you have. People are often thoughtlessly content to live in a "nice" neighbourhood and say carelessly: "Oh, that will do", because they have heard well of (say) Hampstead, Chelsea, Golders Green, or the like. Better consult your own health in relation to the locality. For instance, you may have a tendency to lung-trouble, and Chelsea lies low by the river and has a tendency to damp and fog. That would rule it out for you.

Even much-praised localities have local disadvantages which people generally only take the trouble to find out, not at first but later on, by fretful personal experience. For instance, a certain suburb may have great advantages in an excellent and frequent train-service to London, and similar amenities. But the houses there are on a clay soil, and the walls of the houses are liable to crack, causing unsightliness and expense unless the standard of building is of the very highest order. This is only one instance of showing that it is better to find out by enquiry betimes than by personal experience too late.

Proximity to work is another important factor. In an uncertain world where railway and other accidents occur and where transport may be dislocated by fog or anarchic "strikes", this is worth consideration.

Unthinking people often say: "I work in London (or some other big town). It only takes me an hour (or the like) to get from home to work." They ignore the fact that this adds up to a frightening slice of life, which, if they faced it, might shake their complacency. If they travel by car, the time is lost so far as productive work is concerned, for writing or reading is then out of the question. By train, some productive work may be done by determined effort, but usually it is not. And year after year, the long routine journey becomes boring, wearisome—and what is worse—deadening to body and mind in the extreme.

Will you have a self-contained flat in town? Or a house in the country? One does not necessarily exclude the other, and there may be, of course, the pleasures—and the expenses—of having both at once.

Modern-minded people increasingly refuse to have their lives cluttered up with numerous trifling responsibilities, such as a house-occupation entails. Merely to set out the matters which any house-owner has to deal with in these modern days, is startling. The householder is game for the Inland Revenue (Schedule A) and the Local Authority (rates) to begin with; then come constant repairs of all kinds, from the roof above to the drains below, not to speak of structural alterations, general renewals, and decorations. This is so far as the mere structure is concerned.

To this Mr. House-Owner must add such troubles and responsibilities as accounts and correspondence over electricity, gas, fuel, radio, telephone, television, plumbing, interior decorations, and all those things that a house gives rise to. Supplementary to the house is probably a garage and a garden, with their additional, if incidental, troubles and expenses.

Now if you are a born administrator and organiser, this dealing with necessary trifles may be meat and drink to your spirit. Even if you are not, there may be amenities: such as tranquillity or the facility to keep pets or raise one's own produce or constant fresh air, greenery, and bird-song, that make for you, a house in the country well worth while. You should set advantage against disadvantage, and you may come down on the side, perhaps, of being a house-owner or householder after all.

Or perhaps you look at the problem with a towns-man's eye. The great city such as London has its amenities, too, in the shape of theatres, art-galleries, museums, cinemas, libraries, as well as convenience and saved time in transport. You wish to be a "mobile" personality instead of a "rooted" one, perhaps. And it may well be that a furnished service flat, for which you pay a high inclusive charge, is yet cheaper and more advantageous to you person-ally, and far more trouble-free, than the much-vaunted "house of one's own". It is a question of individual preference.

Again, one man likes to own his personal motor-car. Perhaps he enjoys tinkering with, and cleaning it, and gets a thrill from possession. Moreover, he may use a car so often that rapid availability is well-nigh necessary. His opposite number uses a car perhaps only at fine week-ends; cares nothing for a possessory thrill; hates tinkering or cleaning; and regards with dismay the everlasting bother (as he regards it) of Road Fund licences, insurance certificates, petrol and oil bills, repairs, replacements, depreciation, garaging, and the rest. This citizen will hire a car instead of possessing one—and can congratulate himself on time, trouble, and money saved.

There is no doubt at all that either the inveterate owner or the inveterate hirer, so far as his stationary box or his mobile box is concerned, can make out a very good case for his mode of life. Probably the majority prefer the owned house and car—but that is not to say that they are the wiser. The majority are not always right—even when they are political voters and so deemed to be.

One can only say that it all depends upon your circumstances and taste, and that having regard to these, you should choose your immediate home-environment.

2. Travel

But do not make the cardinal error which most people, and certainly most people in the small British islands do, of under-travelling.

People often say quite untruthfully: "I can't afford to travel. Travel is expensive." The truth is that generally speaking we cannot afford not to travel and to be perpetual stay-at-homes taking one annual holiday. Nor is travel expensive if one takes care to take advantage of cheaper travel and sets down what one gets in return for one's expenditure.

If you travel expensively and insist (as most British people rather strangely do) on extra luxury and on turning a foreign environment into a British environment, or an International hotel environment, travel can indeed cost a lot. But here, as in other fields, your determination can assuage cost-difficulties. It is remarkable how people with little, or even no, money, manage to travel far and wide if they really want to do so.

Not to see a very great deal of the world at first hand for yourself is one of the greatest blunders in life. Yet there are people who actually pride themselves, mistakenly enough, on holidaying in the same British holiday-resort every year for twenty-five, thirty or even more years. For them, the variety and diversity of this Earth, with its different climates, scenes, races, hardly exist—except as a tale in travel-books or a picture on cinema-screens.

Travel abroad not merely gives a broadening and quickening of the mind. It enriches and enlarges the physical experience. It refreshes the spirit jaded by the routine of over-familiar use and want and a narrow cramped environment. It gives memories that are renewed pleasures for the remainder of life.

There are treasures in Rome, Florence, Athens, Madrid, Seville, Lisbon, Paris, Brussels, The Hague, Budapest—to name only a few European cities at random—that can be seen nowhere else. Each of these exhales an atmosphere of its own. You hear of Capri or the Grecian Archipelago, or Java, or Tahiti, the Holy Land of Palestine—or some such place that appeals powerfully to your imagination, and fills you with longing. Instead of putting the longing aside—as most foolish people do—make up your mind to overcome difficulties and go. You will never regret that. But if you do not, you may very well regret *that*.

Nothing, indeed, is commoner than such vain regrets as these, in the evening of life. Remember that the saddest words of tongue or pen are, as Whittier said, "It might have been".

Let me tell you the story of an English boy-waiter in his very early twenties, whom I had known in London and met to my surprise in a hotel on the French Riviera.

"Used you not to wait on me at the Trocadero Restaurant in London?" I asked him.

"Yes, sir. I remember you well. I was a *commis* then."

"So you've taken a holiday-job here for a bit, I suppose?"

"No sir. I live here."

"But you're English. Why do you live here?"

"Because it's the best place to live. I said to myself: 'A waiter has one advantage; he can carry his job on anywhere. Then why not live in the nicest climate and where there are next to no taxes?' So I made enquiries of all the chaps in the waiting game who'd travelled, and they all said 'The French Riviera'. Well, I wasn't satisfied, and asked where do gentlemen go and live in Europe when they've money and can live where they like? I found it was either the French Riviera or near Lisbon. So I went to the

Berlitz school in London, learned a bit of French, and got a job here."

"Are you satisfied?" I asked him.

"I should say so. More money and none taken off you. And a lovely climate. And everybody so good-tempered here. And you don't get worked to death."

"Really?"

"Yes, sir. And I tell you another thing. When a Riviera waiter goes to London for a holiday, he comes back and says 'I'm glad to get back'. But when a London waiter comes here for a holiday, he goes back and says 'I'm sorry to go back'. My dad told me that one, and it's true. I've verified it by experience."

The modern-minded young waiter certainly showed good sense and initiative. There may be people who prefer London to the French Riviera— I suppose the famous Dr. Johnson was of that mind— but whichever you prefer is the place for you, as that youth sensibly had decided.

What folly, then, to allow yourself to be stultified, as many do, in health and pleasure, by the alterable accident of place-environment. It is one of the greatest mistakes in the art of living to live in a place which is uncongenial either to the body or the mind. Often it may be inconvenient to make a change. Sometimes it may be really difficult. But it is never impossible for the ingenious and resolute person.

And I doubt if it is ever too late in life (providing one has one's health and strength) to improve one's place-environment if one is unhappy where one lives.

Even if complete removal should be impossible, as

D•

in some cases owing to one's livelihood, family responsibilities, or the like, it may be a modern outlook finds temporary anodynes. The bicycle, the motor-cycle, the motor-car, the railway train, and the aeroplane, offer splendid possibilities of rapidly changed temporary environment at short notice.

In modern life it is not the facilities, but the energy and enterprise to take advantage of them, that most people lack.

Take care when you travel that you *do* travel indeed. Some introvert people, however far they travel, always remain in the same place, that is to say, within themselves. They are hardly conscious of strange and new surroundings. Now to a certain extent that is inevitably true of all of us, and Oliver Goldsmith has well expressed that truth:

> "Still to ourselves in every place consigned,
> Our own felicity we make or find."

And another, and a greater, poet, has put it even more arrestingly:

> "The mind is its own place,
> And in itself
> Can make a heaven of hell, a hell of heaven."

Here can be realised another benefit of the changing and diversified life given to us by travel: namely, that it tends, as we say, "to take us out of ourselves".

That is no mean or unhealthful blessing at times. For just as we need a rest from other people, there are occasions in life when we need a respite from our routine selves. After all, we are many more selves than our routine selves, or at any rate we have the capacity to be more if we so wish.

Making a very brief précis of this chapter, we find here:

1. Home should be for you, not you for the home. Make your home lest it should make you—what you should not be. Your home should be congenial, like its shell to the snail.

2. Consider whether you are naturally a "mobile" or "rooted" personality, and consider the self-advantages in being a town or country mouse.

3. Do not "under-travel". Travel is never prohibitively expensive. And when you travel take care to get out of yourself and your routine-environment.

CHAPTER VII

THE ENVIRONMENT OF PERIOD

1. Speed and Distraction

Would you particularly like to have lived in the era of the French Revolution?

Probably not. Few moderns would. Looking back on it, from the advantage of having the perspective of these modern days, the French Revolutionary Period in France does not strike one as being one of the Golden Ages of mankind. One does not need to be a contemporary French nobleman or cleric, and take their doubtless prejudiced view of such delights as guillotines, property-confiscation, and exile, to see that the era had its disadvantages.

Yet the poet Wordsworth, who lived in the era, could burst into this lavish panegyric of that period:

> "Bliss was it in that dawn to be alive
> But to be young was very heaven!"

Not all Wordsworth's contemporaries could, or did, agree—though doubtless they thought there had been worse days in the past. The great politician, Edmund Burke, did not share the poet Wordsworth's view, as his *Reflections on the French Revolution* plainly showed. And, after all, what Wordsworth felt was youth, and poetry, and the joy of life, and he would have felt that equally perhaps in our era.

Moreover, people, particularly elderly people, are fond of talking of "the good old days". But "good King Charles's Golden Days" are here and now so far as you and I are concerned. If our days are neither particularly golden nor particularly good, they are, at any rate, as golden and as good as we shall get.

What folly, then, not to make the best of them! With this sentiment everyone will agree—in words. But in practice few people live in their period.

"How can anyone do other?" you may ask.

Very easily. Indeed, all too easily. Most living people, as we have seen, are creatures of routine and habit, and their earlier life persists into their later in many, perhaps, most, cases. The novelty in life, as in thought and ideas, is distrusted and disliked instinctively. The human mind, like the human body, tends to love what is familiar to it.

Occasionally an extreme case draws pointed attention to this human idiosyncrasy. An old man or old woman confesses that he or she, has for long years lived oblivious of the world's happenings. They have lived (except perhaps for newspaper-reading) almost as though they were living in the days of Elizabeth the First, instead of the days of Elizabeth the Second. In brief, 400 years of change have meant almost nothing to them.

Be the child of your age. Keep abreast of the times, and not merely mentally. Many people whose outlook is more or less of their epoch, still act as though modernity were not for them. Keep up-to-date in every way.

Do not imagine that being a child of your day means that you must neglect or forget the past. Not at all. It means that you are the inheritor, or inheritrix, of the past with an eye on the future.

To some extent if you live a busy social life you can hardly escape your period. The telephone, the motor-car, the radio, the television set, the talking three-dimensional film, the Comet air-liner, and the rest, will inevitably impinge upon your attention. But the important thing, of course, is to take full advantage of these advantages so far as you may.

Nor can you escape the note of your period.

For instance, this is an age of speed and haste. You may resolve that you dislike hurry, scurry, and flurry (an excellent mental attitude). But only to a certain extent can you move in modern London life with slow dignity. The rushing omnibuses will not wait. The moving, hurrying throng will not permit you to walk slowly on the crowded pavement. Watch a modern crowd! The pace is fast. Every city-dweller is in desperate haste—even when there is no need to hurry at all!

If you go out East by an aeroplane, the contrast between the slow dignity of even ordinary folk and the hurrying movement of Western folk, comes as a shock. The carriage and composure of even poverty-stricken Eastern women in a city like Cairo or Stamboul, as they walk in quiet dignity along the streets, is altogether admirable. Scrambling, shambling, jostling Western women in London or Manchester, devoid of deportment as they rush about city streets, come very badly out of the comparison.

However, there is no help for it. If poor Eastern women walk like conscious queens and poor Western women like flurried animals, it is because they live in different environments. The note of the West to-day is speed.

Not only in the streets is this observable. Devices in offices and factories speed up the tempo of existence. Doubtless a good deal of the speed is of more apparent than real value, and though work is done faster less is done. For instance, the modern writer has shorthand, typewriting, and even planatyping perhaps, as well as the dictaphone, to help him to increase output. Yet where is the modern playwright or novelist whose life-output exceeds the enormous number of words turned out with a hand-driven quill-pen by Shakespeare, Scott, Dickens, or Trollope? And lengthy works of such quality, too.

Those men worked hard and worked long. They were giants indeed, but we have our giants too, and the life-output of our great writers like Aldous Huxley and Somerset Maugham is very considerable. Yet it is below their predecessors'.

Why? Possibly because this is a period of distraction, as well as of speed. We do not concentrate upon one thing for long periods as our fathers did. Life has far too many complications. There are more and more varied activities, capable of pursuing us wherever we are, home, restaurant, place of work, street, and so on.

Now these distinctively modern notes of speed and distraction have both advantages and disadvantages. One is forced, in order to live effectively in one's period, to attune oneself to them. But one need not sacrifice oneself to them. "Never run after a bus or a woman, there'll be another along in a minute" may be a cynicism, but it has its lesson. Pace can kill. Distraction can be so constant as to drive one distracted, and prevent the doing or thinking of anything worth while.

So, while you are a child of your age, do not forget that there are tendencies in it that, in their exaggerated form, require to be resisted, just as in their advantageous form they require to be accepted.

But, by and large, it comes to this. You cannot live in the past. Nor can you live in the future. Compelled to live in the present—except in imagination from time to time—you must make the best of your epoch, taking every advantage of its benefits and reducing, so far as you can, its discomforts and inconveniences to yourself.

2. Politics and Economics

Clearly discern the tendencies of your period. Calmly appraise them so far as your individual living is concerned. Check book-knowledge and newspaper-pictures by what is clearly happening around you in your day and generation.

There are about $2\frac{1}{2}$ billion fellow-individuals on the earth at this period. There is too little food to nourish adequately all that population, largely owing to modern soil-erosion and sea-poisoning.

Over-population and the lunatic "killing" of the soil and the sea bring land-hunger to the "big" nations. This, together with the idolatry of nationalism, leads to wars and rumours of wars. As a consequence, Governments, whether so-called democratic or totalitarian, hold their populations in an iron grip of control for war-readiness. You, as an individual, will feel that control in an infinite variety of ways, the chief being oppressive taxation (which includes rates) both open and disguised, both direct and indirect.

Just run over in your mind a few of the imposts to which you and your life are likely to be subjected, by a British Government in the present year of grace. You will be astonished and appalled at the total.

For instance, you may pay in life income tax, land-tax, and surtax, general rates and water-rate, a tax on every sum of money you receive, and on every sum of your own you draw out of a bank, on every alcoholic drink you swallow, on every whiff of tobacco you smoke—to give some few obvious instances. There are—literally—hundreds of other taxes on food and goods, to which the citizen is directly exposed, and of course the cost of taxation of others enters into the cost of every necessity and every luxury he procures.

It is depressingly instructive to sit down and endeavour to add up all the special trifling taxes that are exacted from one—and to calculate the bleeding loss of money which I must insist is the loss of life, to which you, an ordinary British citizen, are subjected to-day. Have you a motor-car? Have you a dog? Have you a gun? A wireless set? A television set? Do you eat, drink and smoke? You are directly taxed on these properties and activities. You cannot marry without being taxed. You cannot die without being taxed.

You can, it is true, breathe the air (or "smog") without taxation for each breath you draw—but perhaps by the time these words reach you, some ingenious Government will have provided for that form of taxation. Certainly the water that Providence provides free does not reach you free of charge.

Ordinary British citizens are apt to read of millionaires, peers, and other wealthy persons, in death or life being mulcted of vast sums with equanimity, if not approval. "Let the galled jade wince; our withers are unwrung" is the general attitude. We may leave politicians to argue whether this modern tendency to re-distribute wealth by taxation (as such confiscation is called) is right or wrong. This is not a political treatise and here we are only concerned with modern taxation and its repercussions on the ordinary life of ordinary individuals.

For you must allow for this and take it into consideration. There is no need, and indeed it is almost impossible, to exaggerate this evil. On the other hand, there is no sense in under-estimating it and its effect upon your living-standards, present and future.

The State (and the rest of its sub-creations) is, without doubt, a useful institution so far as it goes. But if it goes too far in its exactions, the citizen may well ask himself whether life under it is becoming less than tolerable. Milking the cow until blood is drawn, is beyond toleration—and that may be the situation, if the future copies the immediate past in Britain, as it may.

For the elder of us there may be no remedy but to stay and bear it. But if you are young, enterprising, and high-spirited, you may consider whether emigration may not be the remedy for you. You may meditate on the reported fact that a Mr. James Gage, an American citizen, left by will a fortune of £60,000 by an English relative on condition he lived in England, decided it was better to give up the fortune and live in the U.S.A. He had lived in England—and preferred to live in the U.S.A.

Well, Mr. Gage may be right or he may be wrong. But we have not yet heard of anyone giving up £60,000 for the privilege of living in the England of to-day. And as a wit said, with our climate, our cooking, and our taxation, it is difficult to visualise anyone doing so. Still, no doubt for the average Briton, the old country is the old country, and it has its attractions, even at the present day.

You must face it, however, that your period has closed, for you, certain abilities to control the future, as strong-minded and ambitious people often desire to do, even from their graves. The Inheritance and Revenue laws now prevent you in many respects from doing as you may wish with your life-acquisitions after death. You cannot "found a family" with the certainty of providing for it to the second, third, or even fourth generation. You may, however, be prepared to put up with the limitations imposed by the current ideas of your period.

To-day, also, is a day of lessened individualism, and greater conventional standardisation. Here again you may find it expedient to conform to the standards of your age.

The rule, and the only rule, that can be given for living in your period is to apply common sense in deciding which tendencies to resist or ignore and which to accept. The motto "When in Rome do as the Romans do" applies not only to place but also to time. You cannot behave like an Ancient Briton, or even an Ancient Roman, in modern Britain (except at a costume-ball, perhaps) with any advantage to yourself, or any edification to your fellows. Speaking generally, it is necessary to be *of* your period, which one day may be known to History as the immediate pre-Atomic age. Worse or better periods may succeed it, but this is a matter for arm-chair speculation. Your concern, it cannot be too strongly insisted upon, is with the here-and-now if you are to live efficiently and effectively and to your own and the world's best advantage. To-day, and no other, is yours for daily use.

To sum up:

1.   "Good King Charles's Golden Days" are here and now. No other days are golden for you. You must live in your day and generation.

2.   To do this, you must be attuned to the atmosphere of your period.

3.   Use modern advantages to the full: mitigate modern disadvantages. In brief, make the best of your period, as of your environment.

4.   This is an age of much speed and many distractions.

5. Clearly observe and calmly appraise, the general, political, and economic tendencies of your age. Use your common-sense so that either with them or against them, you may live efficiently and effectively to your own and the world's advantage.

CHAPTER VIII

STREAMLINING YOUR DAYS AND WAYS

1. The Purposeful Life

WHAT is the purpose and meaning of life in general? Nobody knows. That question has been asked from the beginning of time until the present day. There is no certain answer to it.

Religions and philosophies painfully try to give some answer to that question. The varying answers they purport to give are not conclusive. That is to say, that while the adherents of one particular belief, be it religious or philosophic, may accept the answer of that religion, that brings no general conviction to non-adherents. And most of the answers given are imprecise, tentative, and are based solely on speculation and faith. Even the adherents of one religion or one philosophy are seldom agreed amongst themselves as to the purpose or meaning of life.

It is, however, generally agreed that whatever the ultimate and real purpose and meaning of life in general, these are a mystery hidden from the human intellect. It is thought and felt deeply and sincerely that life must have some purpose and some meaning, but that, in the absence of a blinding revelation, that purpose and that meaning, beyond the obvious one on the surface, which seems to be life-continuance or life-preservation, can be theorised about with no certainty as to the correct answer.

That being so, it is better for most of us for most of the time to eschew speculation upon the insoluble and turn to the easier, more pressing, and more urgent, problem of our individual lives.

Fortunately, for ourselves and our fellows, each of us can give both purpose and meaning to each of our lives. It is imperative and essential that we should do so. The aimless, purposeless, life is of little value to its owner or to others.

Simple considerations of everyday experience show the all-importance of having a purpose in everything. If you shoot aimlessly your missile will hit any-where but the target. If you walk aimlessly you arrive at no objective. One could multiply similar instances.

Now life itself is no exception to this general rule. A life with a purpose has direction and point. It has intelligibility, that is to say, a meaning. It acquires coherence and unity. The life-owner, knowing where he is going, walks in that direction only and with speed, tending to eschew waste of time and effort. He is likely to arrive at his destination because he goes, and keeps on going, in its direction.

Therefore it is important, above all things, to decide early and finally on the main general purpose of your life. It does not so much matter what it is so long as it is worthy of effort, even if not a great and good effort. Thus it may be the attainment of a vast fortune, or brilliant success in your profession or calling, or becoming a saint or hero, or, if you are a woman, the fulfilment of yourself by wifehood, motherhood, and grandmotherhood.

It must not be small and petty and easily attainable. Otherwise it fails to inspire and is quickly exhausted. It must be something worth dedicating a life-time to, and something that calls for a life-struggle.

Once the main aim is decided, everything falls into place and the life-pattern quickly begins to take shape. Each day and every day, in spite of interruptions, digressions, divergences, and set-backs, that are inevitable, the circumstances of human existence being what they are, your life follows its pattern and traces its intricate design.

And this—more than most things—lends interest and value to the routine of living, to the daily round and common task. Nothing gives the life-owner more satisfaction, even if he be not ambitious in the vulgar sense of the term, than to feel he is progressing in the direction he wants to go.

So—choose your purpose, if your purpose has not already chosen *you*. Make up your mind early and definitely. Then go all out. Start your pattern and carry on with it. Don't let "I can't" wait upon "I will", like the poor cat in the adage, as Lady Macbeth said.

This is one of the grand secrets of effective and satisfactory living: the purposive, one-pointed life.

It is not my business—or anyone else's—to dogmatise upon what *your* purpose in life should be. But it is a high aim that it should not be altogether worldly and material; it should have at the very least a touch of mysticism, romance, elevation, poetry, religion (or all these) about it. Thus, if you intend to become Lord High Chancellor of England, or Archbishop of Canterbury, or Prime Minister, these glittering prizes are not sufficiently golden in themselves. A Biblical text is in point here: The Deity "gave them their desire and sent leanness withal into their souls". Your punishment might be to attain your ambition and become a laughing-stock of a Chancellor, a disastrous Primate, or a discredited Premier. It is not much being numbered amongst the Twelve Apostles if your name is Judas Iscariot.

And do not imagine that your End is all. More important than the arrival is the travelling. "To travel hopefully is a better thing than to arrive" as Robert Louis Stevenson sensibly said. (Though there is joy in arrival too.) Nor need you imagine that failure to reach your End is failure in living.

Thus a writer who writes well and to the purpose, need not (and probably will not) worry that he is not Shakespeare; a climber of many peaks need not mourn that he has not attained the summit of Everest; the discoverer of a minor mathematical truth, that he is neither Newton nor Einstein, and so on. It is enough that we follow faithfully our nature and our business. This, and this only, is the great thing.

And, after all, the very greatest of human kind can do no more.

The present "Grand Old Man" of English literature, Mr. W. Somerset Maugham, often and deservedly quoted in this book, early found his purpose in life. He decided that he wanted to make a pattern of his existence, and he did so. Having so done, in his old age it occurred to him naturally enough, he being a writer, to make a book of it, which he did, and called the book *The Summing Up*.

As he had thought much, read much, and experienced more, this book has great merit. And how did this modern writer sum up his conclusion upon the whole? At the very end of the book he quotes Fray Luis de Leon: "The beauty of life, he says, is nothing but this, that each should act in conformity with his nature and his business."

That really is right living.

2. Jumbled and Muddled Existence

Once you have your purpose and your pattern, it is relatively easy to streamline your days and ways towards the predestined goal. To a certain extent the very existence of purpose and pattern does it for you.

Do not be discouraged because you do not shoot like a rocket to your goal. Do not be dismayed because you loiter and digress from the path, you being the fallible thing you undoubtedly are. Fall by the wayside, unless your will is of steel, you almost certainly will. This is not failure. The great thing is that you should pick yourself up and go on.

Best progress is achieved by the plodding tortoise rather than the spurting hare. Slowness does not matter providing it is accompanied by steady, relentless perseverance. Hold fast to your purpose, and achieve progress towards it.

But perhaps you are not convinced that the purposive life is the best. Destitute of any personal aim or bent, inactive but contemplative, you wonder whether life is not merely to be lived as it comes, without its being consciously forced by you, the life-owner, in any one direction. Seeing no purpose in life in general, perhaps you doubt the efficacy of providing one for your own life in particular.

That certainly is a point of view.

Once I knew such a man and had him as a friend. I could write of him quite truly as Gray wrote of others such: "Along the cool, sequester'd vale of life, they kept the noiseless tenor of their way". He lived in the pleasant city of Chester and (strangely enough, considering his temperament and tone) he was a journalist. Exactly what you would not expect a journalist to be like, and very unlike most of his craft! Yet a very efficient journalist, too.

Serene, unhurried, remote, withdrawn, he moved amongst men, things, and events, reminding me of Hamlet's friend Horatio, who was "not passion's slave". Ironically yet not deeply amused, clear-sighted, interested yet not concerned, he contemplated the spectacle of existence on the basis of one who sees, thinks, and feels, yet is not called on to act or even write what he saw, thought, or felt, being only engaged to live and do his daily duties.

Neither what is called a success nor what is called a failure in life, he was in the late sixties what he was in the late twenties, except physically. Seeing him after a thirty-years' interval, I, who admired this rare spirit greatly, could not help exclaiming to myself, in the Robert Browning tag: "What porridge had John Keats?"

Certainly he had no purpose in life beyond living. Given his temperament, he was justified, for he fulfilled the true beauty of Life according to the doctrine of de Leon, living in conformity with his nature and his business. Yet I am disposed to wonder whether "his business" might not have been done better and more nobly if he had had "the purpose ribbed and edged with steel"—and some of his journalism have turned into literature.

If you are one of this admirable kidney, it may be that without a definite specific purpose in life beyond a general "living in conformity with your nature and business", you have attained—for yourself—the art of right living. Natural contemplatives like you and my friend are rare spirits indeed; let us not under-rate their worth.

But contrast the active purposive life and the contemplative life with a very different order of existence.

Take, for instance, Frederick Dickens, of whom you have probably never heard, of whom little is known, and of whom nothing would be remembered were he not the brother of that tremendous human spirit, Charles Dickens. Seldom in life can there have been a more purposeful, energetic, and determined man than Charles Dickens, not only in his chosen craft but in life generally. But when Frederick, the last surviving brother, died in 1868, Charles, who had expended himself and his substance generally upon this brother (as upon others of his sponging, needy relatives) and who had affection for him yet knew him untrustworthy, wrote:

"It was a wasted life. But God forbid that one should be hard upon it or upon anything in this world that is not deliberately and coldly wrong."

A terrible epitaph indeed! A wasted life. And recorded—with kindly extenuating words—by the generous and affectionate brother who was so ready to shoulder crushing family burdens. There is nothing known of Frederick Dickens—the son of Micawber—that suggests he was not as shiftless as Dickens *père*.

One does not know enough to judge—and one can only accept the verdict.

But the very words make the heart bleed. Life ought not to be wasted. Yet there are lives, promising and bright at dawn, of which, with the kindest will in the world, one can find nothing better to say than this.

And, in addition, many lives that appear to be successful on the surface may be, in reality, wasted lives.

So many lives never really find themselves or know themselves. Nor is this the case only amongst the lowly and ignorant. Many well-educated persons lead jumbled and muddled lives—very often because they are, like Martha in the Gospel-story, "so careful and troubled about many things" that they neglect "the one thing needful", which is attention to their own life. It is frequently a case of not seeing the forest for the trees.

In childhood, and perhaps even in youth, it is natural not to be able to apprehend as a whole the bewildering and novel phenomenon of life with its constant impact on the sensitive senses. It overwhelms by its novelty and strangeness, its variety and bulk. But in manhood and womanhood, one should be used to it. There is no excuse for not being familiar with it all by the time one is thirty, or even earlier. To be incapable in adult life of grappling with the anarchy and chaos of daily life as they present themselves, and reducing them to order, is to have remained a child too long.

No one would live in a house from which the filth and rubbish were never removed, but left to accumulate and overwhelm every atom of space, like the manure of the Augean stables. Then why live a life clogged and cluttered up by its own excrement? Rather have a ruthless spring-cleaning from time to time. Relentlessly cut off and fling away what is useless and frustrating. Remorselessly refuse to permit the theft of your days and ways by what is alien to them.

No matter under what pretence or pretext your life is stolen from you, or buried and stifled under a mountain of extraneous matters, do not tolerate it. That the claims of others are insistent, one knows only too well. Nevertheless, in so far as they are exaggerated, they must be resisted.

Between the claims of the State and other authorities, the claims of employment or other livelihood, the claims of social life, the claims of relatives and friends, nay, even the claims of total strangers and bodies organised or unorganised, you may come to have no real life of your own. Even if you are what is called a public man or woman, these claims have to be reduced to manageable proportions.

Equally, your own fritterings, follies, idlings, and the like, have to be rigidly curtailed. In this matter of loss, we are often our own worst enemies. Do not overlook this aspect of the matter.

Order, neatness, symmetry, and fitness, are great things in themselves. They are the result of skill, knowledge, and care. You admire them in the furnishings of a room, in clothing worn upon the person, in the perfection of any piece of work made or done. Equally admirable and desirable are they in the conduct of life itself.

To bring muddled, jumbled, half-realised life into order, discipline, and beauty, means that you are on the way not only to self-conquest but also to conquer the world of persons and things that hem your life in on every side.

Let us look at some practical steps by which this may be done.

3. Streamlining

You know what streamlining means. This is the process you, in pursuit of your life-purpose and the pattern of your life-plan, have to carry out.

Take, first, the ground-stuff of life which is Time. And time, remember, in a strictly limited rationed quantity, as we have already seen.

The day is a convenient unit to deal with, for many obvious reasons. It has not twenty-four hours in it for your conscious purposes. But it should have sixteen at least—giving you eight hours sleep and rest, which is generous and ample and errs, if at all, for most of us on the side of too much.

Arnold Bennett once wrote a book called *How to Live on 24 Hours a Day*. It sold better, he tells us in his *Journal*, than any other of his books. And it may be of value to you.

Of the sixteen hours, perhaps eight or less are devoted to your livelihood and activities incidental and ancillary to that livelihood, such as travelling. What of the remaining eight hours?

Sit down with paper and pencil. Stringently analyse how you spend that time. Do it with rigid accuracy. You may be able to account for every hour in detail of the day on which you carry out this exercise. Possibly you will not be able to account exactly for each lost hour of the previous day. Most probably, still less will you be able to account at all for many expended hours of the previous day before that.

As for the forgotten expended hours of last week . . . the less said the better!

Gone beyond recall! No matter. Life begins afresh each day. Having done the exercise to-day, do the same to-morrow, and again the next morrow. In four or five days—certainly in a week—you will have enough data to work upon.

Now you have a picture—probably a disturbing and disconcerting picture—of how you have lost, dribble by dribble, moments and hours which would add up to weeks, months, and years, in the course of a lifetime, of your precious heritage of life. You have fribbled and frittered away, or let others do it, what you could have used and expended to your benefit.

From realising this situation is but a step to the remedying of it. Cut out the waste. Make effective use of the surplus. That is to say, use it for the attainment of your purpose.

(By the way, in passing, it is no bad idea to apply this exercise to your expenditure of money as well as the expenditure of your life-time. Equally, the picture obtained may be a disconcerting and salutary one leading to a resolve to fool away no more, or much less, cash).

But note, that in order that the exercise may fully benefit you, you must carry it out with rigid honesty. Every amount of time or money must be accounted for. Act as uncompromisingly as if you were an auditor or accountant or Income Tax inspector examining fraudulent accounts, for the purpose of giving sworn evidence about them in Court.

Perhaps the money-state makes you resolve to keep exact accounts in a cash-book for the future so as to keep a check on foolish expenditure. Excellent! Many people do this. But equally excellent, why not keep an account-book of your time-expenditure so that you can keep a watch and check on this? Few people do this.

One who did was Anthony Trollope, the novelist, to whom I have already alluded. If he failed to keep up to his stated daily programme, there was the record to reproach him and to oblige him to work longer and

E

harder on a later day, to rectify the loss. When he failed, the sight of his record was "a blister to my eye and a sorrow to my heart", he records. Naturally failure became rarer and was always compensated for in such circumstances.

Here at the grave risk of seeming platitudinous to the younger generation, let me put in a word on the virtue of early rising. Young people hate it. Also they have heard about it before, and despise the admonition. I have been young myself and it took me thirty years to believe in the sovereign virtues of this prosaic and uncomfortable habit.

If you are in earnest, adopt it.

It was this simple habit, rigidly carried out unswervingly over the long years, that brought both the Trollope novelists to wealth and success. The elder Mrs. Trollope achieved her colossal output of 114 books between the late ages of 56 and 72, and kept her dying husband and dying children in comfort, on that work, and did it all (as her son records) each day before the household rose from bed. Trollope, who might have been an ordinary respectable Civil Servant and forgotten as such, made himself immortal by the novels he wrote before breakfast, morning after morning.

That, you must agree, is impressive. It strikes home.

It shows plainly how to streamline your days so that a purpose may be carried on to fruitfulness and how production can be achieved and maintained.

Now for your way or habits. These must be streamlined to efficiency also.

For good or ill, we are the creatures of habit. It is of paramount importance that those habits should be good ones.

Regular and simple habits are best for body and mind. Your strictly ordered day, already achieved, will help to force regularity of habit upon you. Regular hours of sleep, of food, of work, or recreation, lead not only to efficiency of the body-mind machine but also to its wearing quality of long life.

Many bad habits, seemingly trifling, become of deepest consequence, especially when persisted in over long periods. Over-eating, over-drinking, over-smoking, are insidious but very real dangers, and are generally known and recognised as such by the world at large. But small irregular snacks, frequent occasional drinks, too-strong or poor and adulterated tobacco the cleanliness of which is uncertain, are less recognised as dangers to health and welfare. Dyspepsia, cirrhosis of the liver, and infective disease, have been scientifically traced to these habits.

And there are other bad mental habits, seemingly as innocuous as these bodily habits, which are not less dangerous in their ill-effects.

Then the habit of merely putting things down thoughtlessly instead of obeying the tiresome child-hood-injunction of "Always put a thing in its right place and nowhere else". The loss of time and expense of vexation in trying to find a mislaid object—some-times in haste—can be very afflicting, and the punishment is often disproportionate to the trifling nature of the offence. Or take the bad habit of leaving a car, taxi, train, room or any other temp-

orary abiding-place, without looking round before
leaving to see that nothing is left behind.

How many hundreds of thousands of people have
this bad habit is shown by the annual statistics of the
Lost Property Office in London alone! If you want
another illustration, go and watch the woe-begone
little queue waiting to reclaim their lost articles at
Waterloo, Victoria, or any other metropolitan
railway-station.

What converted me to the swift streamlined habit
of a backward glance before finally leaving anywhere,
was many painful experiences of time and valuable
property lost, and the advice of a burglar. This
sensible criminal told me: "I always look round
before leaving, to see if I've left anything. The first
house I burgled I forgot to take half the property I'd
collected—and, worse, left my finger-prints behind
as well. That cost me twelve month's imprisonment.
And when I came out, my mother says, 'Serves you
right for being so careless. I always did tell you
about that when you were a boy'."

No doubt the mother did. Mothers generally do.
But it is not what we are told that teaches many of us
but the bitter experience we get in life from ignoring
what we have been told.

Absent-mindedness, while engaged in some practical doing, is attributed to professors and other
intellectual people. But it is widespread amongst all
kinds of people. It has its amusing and endearing
side. But it can be a nuisance and annoyance, and
worse, to its voluntary victim. It is not funny, for
instance, to arrive at a railway station some miles

STREAMLINING YOUR DAYS AND WAYS 133

from home and then recall you have forgotten (while thinking of something else) to lock up the house, or turn off the electric heater, or something similarly disastrous.

The right habit is of course: "Give full attention to what you do at the time you do it."

Unpunctuality is another evil habit. So, too, by the way, is its extreme opposite, which is less generally reprobated, however. I mean a fussy over-punctuality which leads some foolish people to arrive long before the appointed hour, exclaiming: "We have nice time." Punctuality is worth cultivating. Not only is it polite: it saves annoyance and loss, often to your neighbour as well as to yourself.

And, as we all know, even a second's unpunctuality when one has to catch a train, boat, or plane, may be punished very heavily.

Acting in small doings, impulsively, precipitately, and without consideration, often takes toll of effort and time. Your brain will often save your legs, and arms too, if you think even for a second beforehand over what you are about to do.

It is impossible to list all the good habits that you should acquire and all the bad habits you should eschew. What is important is that your attention should be directed to the advantage of good, and the disadvantage of ill, habits in life, and that you should act on the knowledge you acquire by keeping a vigilant watch on your habits and their consequences.

Let us now concisely sum up the chief lessons from this Chapter:

Life, whatever its general purpose and significance, which is a mystery hidden from human cognisance, can be given a purpose and meaning by you and for you.

Resolve to lead a purposive life.

Decide your life's chief aim. Then the pattern of your living will fall into shape as your life is directed to its aim.

This is the first great secret of effective and efficient living, i.e. Live to some purpose.

Take care the purpose is not petty or merely material. Have a touch of the mystic, the romanticist, or the saint about you.

Remember that the travelling is no less important to you than the attainment of your destination.

It may be enough to "live in accordance with your nature and business"—if you are untainted by ambition.

The contemplative life may be as noble, or nobler, than the active life which "gets somewhere".

Ruthlessly clear and clean your life from muddle and jumbles, the exaggerated claims upon it by others and your own follies.

In brief, streamline your days and ways.

As to your days, control the expenditure by ascertaining and recording it. Similarly, your money-expenditure. Cut out waste. Make effective use of the surplus.

As to your ways, control your habits. Some good and bad habits of body and mind analysed with their consequences.

CHAPTER IX

PAST, PRESENT AND FUTURE

1. The Past

IT is an instructive and elevating thing to contemplate life in general and your own life in particular as a whole, its ast, present and future, although we have previously stressed the need of living in the present.

Take the Past first.

History and biography are deeply interesting subjects. But fascinating as these are, your own history and biography are even more fascinating and no less instructive. We are apt to forget our insignificant, helpless, and dependent beginning. We know from hearsay that we were once babies at the breast or bottle, or both, and then crawling, puling, infants, attaining cognisance of our surroundings by slow degrees. We do not in detail remember these stages. Perhaps it would be of little benefit if we could.

But of early childhood, one or two memories remain. These may, almost certainly they must, have been of great import at the time, otherwise they would hardly remain etched upon the tablets of the mind when so many other happenings have been forgotten. However, existent though they be, there probably is little significance in them now.

But of later childhood, perhaps, and certainly of youth, we have abundant memories. And from then onward, there are what seem to be an infinite amount of "Remembrance of Things Past" until this present day.

From this treasure-trove we are always drawing riches for our daily sustenance if we are wise. The lessons, pleasant and unpleasant, that old Experience has taught us, are easily the most valuable and best-assimilated. By living, and in living, we learn.

It is salutary, then, to recall the past from time to time. The young seldom do. Their eyes are fixed eagerly upon what they deem to be the future, but that may be only an illusion. For the real future, possibly by a merciful dispensation, is hidden from us all.

Nor do those in middle-age spend much regard upon the past, though they are less oblivious to it than the young. Their minds in general are steadily occupied by the present with which they are deeply engaged in struggling. Necessity keeps their attention upon to-day, though now and again they may glance before and after, when they have time and opportunity to do so.

But it is well-known how old age tends to look fondly and often over the past. Phrases like: "Things are not what they were", and "In my young days——", and "Things go from bad to worse", are often on the lips of ageing men and women. They turn from the present with readiness and from the future with doubt (realising, perhaps, how little of it is for them) and concentrate with Marcel Proust upon the "Remembrance of Things Past".

This is all very natural. And being according to nature, it is understandable and as it should be. There is no need to deprecate this natural tendency as such.

To repeat words already quoted, Disraeli really summed up this natural tendency when he declared: "Youth is a blunder; Manhood a struggle; Old Age a regret". The blunder of youth is to mistake the mirage of its future for reality: the struggle of manhood is in earning a living for present and future; the regret of old age is for the past as being past and for its sorrows and errors that cannot be rectified.

But natural as all this is, sometimes it becomes exaggerated, and to that extent unnatural. Then it calls for self-correction.

Now of the three periods, it may be asserted safely that the past is least important, and yet perhaps the least dangerous. All the periods have their dangers, it is true. But the past is beyond its own cure. It is also beyond its own self-redemption. Like spilt milk, there is no use in crying over it or wishing it were otherwise.

"Let the dead bury its dead", therefore, is a good motto to apply to the past. The past is indeed dead. It can only be cured, redeemed, raised to life, by the present and future. This is a truth well worth remembering and acting upon, by all of us in all stages of life; in youth, in adult manhood, or womanhood, or in old age.

Resurrected by itself instead of by the present or future, the Past rises from its grave as a spectre in cerements, not as a risen and glorious Body as though in the final Easter Day. It haunts, and perhaps

E*

terrifies, the beholder. Laden with sorrows and sins, it reproaches us, for it is the ghost of its former self. It is better left to corrupt in the earth to which it belongs while we turn from it to the living Present and the unborn Future.

This does not mean that our Past should be forgotten altogether. Indeed, far from it. It can be remembered at times with advantage. But it does mean that the Past should not be brooded upon; not too often nostalgically invoked; not allowed to inhibit us.

Let me give some concrete examples.

Fooled and frittered away money, have you, in the past? Idled away time, have you? Missed chances? Neglected opportunities? Failed or wronged the dead? Fallen short of your ideals, ideas, and resolves? Made a mess of things? Played the fool or the rogue?

How shattering it is to dwell on these things! How discouraging and even despairing!

But—here, before you, in your hands and before your eyes, stands the Present, and, behind her, the Future. They stand ready to redeem the Past, if only you will allow them to do so.

It is never too late. A misspent youth does not necessarily mean a wrecked and ruined life. Nor does a wasted manhood or womanhood. Even at the very last, the end may redeem the beginning and the middle. Some have died nobly and well who never lived nobly and well, like Sidney Carton.

Even though the Past is glorious, it may be better not to recall it too much or too vividly when one, later in life, perhaps has "fallen on evil days". To do so often increases sorrow by a bitter contrast. Unless, indeed, the Past brings comfort and consolation—and it cannot be denied that there are cases where it may, as when one recalls the happiness shared with one loved and lost, for example, or where the old warrior recalls his victories—it is better not recalled too much or too often.

So, upon the whole, I repeat, let the Past lie. This was the advice of a great surgeon, the late Sir William Osler, to the young men of his profession when in an address on his own "Way of Life" he essayed to teach them how to live.

Each day is a new day. We live from day to day. We have to. No day repeats his fellow. There is always hope. Then why brood upon what has gone beyond remedy? Rather look to the Present and then beyond the Present, to the Future.

2. The Present

The Present is Here and Now. This being so, it seems impossible that any living human being should neglect it. Yet many of us, can and do, to our great disadvantage.

We have seen, in treating of the Past, how Youth, hopeful, optimistic, eager, forward-looking Youth, is apt to gaze dazzled at the mirage of the Future. "To-morrow we Live" was the deceitful motto of a European political movement making a special appeal to the young. It was a deceitful motto because to-morrow we may not live at all: none can tell; and because it is to-day that we live.

The Present, indeed, is all we have. A sobering thought, yet a salutary one. Let us not neglect it for its own sake (and incidentally our own) and also because it is the parent of the Future from which we hope so much.

Our day with its note of urgency and haste in the tempo of civilised existence, is peculiarly apt to make us forget that we live in the present. Yet it is with present things and present people and present events that we have to deal.

And yet—all-important as the Present is above the Past, and even above the Future—it is a terrible mistake to do, as some do, and sacrifice the present entirely to the future. That the present should, and must, have regard—even great regard—to the future, just as a mother must have regard to her child, is very true. But there is a limit here.

That limit should be observed.

For the future may never come at all. Or when *a* future comes it may be very different from what is anticipated. To-be-going-to-live and not to have lived is ironic indeed.

Do not, then, entirely sacrifice the present to the future. Pascal, the great French writer, has a passage on this worthy of study. He says: "Of the present we think hardly at all, and if we do it is only that we may draw from it a light to control the future . . . the future alone is our end. Thus we never live; but we hope to live, and it is inevitable that ever-preparing to be happy we never are." Yet to sacrifice something of the present may be wise and necessary.

To spare money to-day for the necessities of spending to-morrow, is an obvious instance. So, too, to sacrifice some modicum of pleasure to-day for the greater pleasures of to-morrow. To study in youth instead of sporting with Amaryllis in the shade in order that one may be armed and well-qualified for the battles of livelihood in adulthood, is a prudent and sensible course of behaviour. Other instances will readily spring to mind, too, all pointing in the same direction.

We should, then, particularly cultivate an awareness, a vivid and alert awareness, of each moment in the present with all our five senses. To do so, according to Walter Pater, is success in life: not to do it is to have failed. In the magnificent "conclusion" to his "Studies in the History of the Renaissance", he urges us to a life of constant and eager observation by all the senses:

"Every moment, some form grows perfect in hand or face; some tone on the hills or the sea is choicer than the rest; some mood of passion or insight or intellectual excitement is irresistibly real and attractive to us—for that moment only. Not the fruit of experience but experience itself is the end. A counted number of pulses only is given to us of a variegated, dramatic life. How may we see in them all that is to be seen in them by the finest senses? How shall we pass most swiftly from point to point, and be present always at the focus where the greatest number of vital forces unite in their purest energy?

"To burn always with this hard, gemlike flame, to maintain this ecstasy, is success in life."

That passage, eloquent and true, is deservedly

famous. But like much that is true and splendid, Pater's vision is not the whole truth. Being human and imperfect, we cannot always burn either with a hard gemlike flame, or at all. We are often flickering in the draughts of circumstance or our own fatigue, listlessness, or ill-health, and sometimes almost extinguished to a faint spark. And both experience and its fruits are the end of living. Pater speaks as a hedonist and an Epicurean, but life, being what it is, beauty, joy, and glory, are not the whole of life.

Still, Pater has much to teach us in this passage on how to regard the present, enjoying it in the best and highest sense, getting "by a quickened, multiplied consciousness" as many pulsations as possible into the brevity that is ours.

Indeed, the wise use of the present is a great part of the art of life. This wise use forbids the bad habit of procrastination—which may be defined as putting-off and mortgaging the future to the present.

The platitudinous motto, "Never put off till to-morrow what you can do to-day" is undervalued. This is probably for the reason that the real evils of procrastination are unrealised. "What does it matter," argues the unconvinced, "if I have plenty of time to-morrow? I may just as well put it off."

Alas! if you do, the procrastination has a mental effect. If postponement were all! It is not. Hesitate and postpone even a small matter, and what happens? An uneasiness, purely psychological, arises and gnaws at the mind. The mental tranquillity is impaired. And—strangely enough—when the morrow comes, one tends to hesitate again, and to hesitate still more.

Why?

Impossible to say, yet it is so: the human mind behaves like that. The small matter magnifies in the mind. Reluctance to act grows and strengthens. Often the postponed act is never done—and a thousand excuses are invented to explain and justify the inaction.

Therefore—act in the present. Never postpone, except for good strong cause. Jump your fences as they come, and you surmount obstacles with ease. Baulk at them, and they soon appear bigger and eventually insurmountable. Vacillation and inaction, like devils, enter into you.

Nor is this the whole evil of procrastination. It affects, often enough, bodily as well as mental health. Does this sound far-fetched? It isn't. The habit of procrastination, which tends to cause, first, faint unease in the mind, turns to worry, and then to neurasthenia. And that is an enemy of happiness, health, and efficient life.

Acting now enables you to retain harmony and equanimity of mind.

Therefore regard procrastination as a deadly sin against life. Use the present for all that pertains to it, and do not mortgage the future.

If you utilise the present to the full, you will have no fears for the future or regrets for the past.

3. The Future

The right way to regard the future is to pay a reasonable regard to it, but not to pay too much regard to it. In modern times, and in Western climes, it is impracticable to "take no thought for the morrow". (This adjuration of Christ's may not have been meant as a permanent admonition to those to whom it was not directly addressed at the time it was uttered.)

We must in youth sacrifice some pleasures of the present in studying to qualify for the future of adulthood. In time of maximum earning-power we must save for the possible future rainy-day. And so on. This is common prudence.

But, on the whole, speaking by and large, the future may be left to take care of itself.

It may never come. Or, as already has been said, if and when it comes, it may be very different from its advance-shadow. Think of the millions of young men, in a thousand varied peaceable occupations, suddenly and unexpectedly changed into uniformed soldiers with weapons in 1914 and again in 1939.

However, the future holds one unquestionable certainty and some very likely probabilities. After all, we do know the general course of human life. It is that we are born; we rise through infancy, childhood, and youth to maturity; we continue for a time on a level, or more accurately, on a seeming level of adulthood, then drop down through old age, and decrepitude, into death.

And death—in spite of all our attainments in atomic physics; conflicting ideologies in politics and economics; our Welfare States; supersonic speed in air-travel; and hope of travel amongst the planets—is exactly as it was for the first savage ape-man. It is the end of the individual. And its precursors may be physical weakness or mental decay, or both.

Death is an unchanged, and unchangeable, fact. And old age is still for us what it was for our ancestors —a period of slowing down, an experienced decline of bodily and mental regression.

It does none of us any good not to face up to these tragic facts. We may pretend otherwise: many people do. But ultimately the facts must be faced. It follows, then, that preparation should be made, while preparation can be made and so far as it can be made, for a state of affairs that the future holds for most of us.

True, it is still what Dr. Samuel Johnson wrote over 200 years ago:

> "How small of all that human hearts endure,
> That part which laws or kings can cause or cure."

Only for "kings" you must write "governments" or even "our fellow-men". There is the unendurable in our own bodies and minds, irrespective of the impacts of others of our kind upon them. As Shakespeare told us: "We must endure our going hence as our coming hither."

The basic fact of personal death in the future, sooner or later, may well prevent over-much worry over the public, social, political, or economic movements, of the nation or the race. Militaristic or industrialised totalitarianism, or both, or some worse technique of government, may be the shape of things to come. But we can only affect by our thoughts, words, and actions, the facts of contemporary history, and that, as units in a vast population (unless we are exceptional individuals or in a position of responsibility) very little indeed.

Another effect which the realisation of the inevitability of our personal decline and our inevitable end, should have upon us is to teach us the transitoriness and comparative worthlessness, against the cosmic backgrounds of the Universe and Eternity, of all we have and are. It teaches us to regard our gifts and possessions as trust-property of which we are only the temporary custodians rather than permanent owners. In the grave is neither personality nor property. We neither are, nor have, any more.

Religion, or philosophy, or both, will teach us how to prepare for death, but their wide fields are beyond the scope of this book. But preparation for old age is a matter for common-sense. The first thing to ensure is that one shall have the comfort and care old age especially needs. The next is to see that tranquillity of mind and body are assured. A long earning-life (by pension, purchased Government or other annuity, insurance, or savings, or by the gratitude of our children, or a combination of all or some of these) should provide food, shelter, clothing, and the few comforts and luxuries that one needs in the declining years.

But even these are not enough. Like the rest of life, old age needs interests. The old person who has something to occupy his or her body-mind pleasurably, is likely to live and flourish till the natural end. So if you have a light occupation, such as books to read, a garden to tend, a collection to increase, light social activities to pursue, or anything of a similar kind, you are well provided for in old age. The miserable—and often the fatal—thing is to retire from the only work you are capable of and care about, and are habituated to, when you have nothing to replace it, and to spend bored unhappy days fretting and pining over your uselessness. Old people reduced to such a parlous condition rarely last long after retirement.

"What shall I do with my old age?" is a sensible question to ask and to answer in early manhood or womanhood. You may, indeed, like some others, wish and hope to "die in harness" as the saying is. That is to say, to work to the end "until the night cometh when no man can work". Well and good, if so you wish. But be prepared for a state of affairs, such as the loss of health or strength, or the decay of some essential faculty such as sight or hearing, which may prevent your doing so.

As an exercise, sum up the contents of this chapter for yourself.

CHAPTER X

GETTING THE BEST, SECOND BEST—
OR WORSE

1. General Considerations

IT is a good general rule in life: Get the best of anything. People are apt to say: "I cannot afford it." But the truth is that we cannot afford anything less than the best—because the second-best or something worse than that is, in the long term and in a sensible view, so much more expensive. Often, the best is cheapest in the long view.

And in considering expense, more than the money paid has to be taken into the reckoning. There is the expense of spirit involved in the disappointment, and the annoyance, and the re-purchase, when the cheap and shoddy article wears out, or lets its obtainer down. Then, too, there is the dissatisfaction involved in knowing that what one has got for oneself is of inferior quality.

Arnold Bennett, the author, used to have a saying: "The best is good enough for me." You may adopt it, to your advantage. It is a good general guide.

But of the best, people do not merely say: "I cannot afford it." They also, or instead, argue: "This"—by which they mean something other than the best—

"will do." But generally it won't—for the reasons already given.

Besides, it is a duty you owe both to yourself and to those who produce the best, to keep the best going. If people of discrimination, culture, and taste, do not uphold the standard of "the best", there quickly arises a degradation of standards. The second or third rate is often produced and pushed, on the plea that people don't want the best.

Do not confound "the best" necessarily with "the most expensive". Not always do the two coincide; though often they do. For example, Java crocodile skin is the best and most expensive of leathers, and is excellent for many purposes. But not for all. Sealskin is lighter, pleasanter, and better-looking, and will last nearly as long, for other purposes. And a suit-case is better made of neither of these, for crocodile is too heavy for air-travel and a world where porters are not always available, and sealskin is not hard-wearing enough to stand rail and steamer hardships.

Similarly, the hair of the little South American vicuña is the best and rarest wool in the world. It is, at the time of writing, fabulously expensive. A real vicuña dressing-gown will cost £75; an overcoat £100. (But they are worth the money.) But vicuña, although the "best" that this world knows, is yet not suitable, and therefore not the best, for under-clothes.

And do not be so unsophisticated as to imagine that the most advertised or most fashionable article is the best. It very seldom is.

Above all, in seeking the best, you need to

educate yourself to perceive fine distinctions. To the ordinary person, something made of gold is gold. But you will ask, "Is it 9-carat, 18-carat, or 22-carat gold?" and esteem it accordingly. You will look at the hall-mark to know (1) who made it; (2) in what town; (3) at what date. Similarly with silver. And similarly with everything else.

The constant analysis and questioning of whatever is presented to you, whether it be a person, a material thing, or an immaterial thing (such as an argument or situation, for instance) will prevent you from being cheated or misled. It makes every activity of life more interesting. And it both stimulates, strengthens, and refines, the mind in one operation.

A questioning, analytical mind is a great weapon in life. You can acquire it. This is entirely a matter of habit. Observe keenly. Pay attention. Question everything until you thoroughly understand it.

And in order that you may understand, you must respect and have regard to the specialist. Remember that every man or woman, however humble, is a specialist in his own particular field, and able, probably, to give you exceptional information of value. "Everybody is good for something" said Lord Chesterfield. "An able man will by dexterity elicit something worth knowing of every being he talks to." Certainly he may.

A friend of mine decided to apply the maxim, "Choose the best" to his study of Comparative Religion at Oxford University. He set down in writing the eleven major religions of the world, and studied them intensively not only in their sacred books, but also by writing to, and in some cases speaking with, prominent protagonists of each religion.

The eleven major religions he found are as follow: Buddhism; Christianity; Confucianism; Hinduism; Islam; Jainism; Judaism; Shintoism; Sikhism; Taoism; and Zoroastrianism.

When my friend commenced his investigations, he was a Western Christian, and a convinced adherent of the Church of England in which he had been brought up. He expected no other result from his dispassionate and impartial studies than that his adherence to Christianity would be confirmed.

The result was far different from his expectations— and, I may add, my own. He became a Buddhist, after nearly two years' intensive study of the eleven religions, which he thoroughly studied.

I will not presume to criticise or question his judgment. It may, or may not, be that the personal factor always, in spite of our own utmost efforts to be impartial, detached, and dispassionate in our enquiry into any such problems as religion, politics, economics, psychology, or the like, enters into the result.

Briefly, my friend's case for his choice of religion was that on a sober and impartial comparison, made (as he said) "without prejudice", pure Buddhism was the noblest of religions in as much as it held out no promises either of reward or punishment to mankind; that in it virtue was its own and only reward; that it believed in no supernatural Being or Beings; that it required no priest or temple; and, above all, that it respected life even in its humblest forms and forbade the killing of any living sentient creature. Such, as I remember it, was briefly his series of conclusions.

Whether he was right or wrong, I do not care to judge, especially as he did not claim to be right in this matter for everyone. He only claimed to be right for himself. And, indeed, he was at pains to point out that every one of the eleven major religions of the world adhered to the Golden Rule: "Whatsoever ye would that men should do to you do ye even so to them."

I give my friend's case merely as an interesting example of an unusual use of the application of the maxim, "Choose the best".

Another interesting example of applying the rule to a situation is furnished by Sir Winston Churchill, according to a Prime Minister of Canada, Mr. Laurent. Laurent reports Churchill as advising him: "Never stand when there is an opportunity to sit down, and and never sit down when you can lie down." An old man's view, it may seem, but it enshrines a great principle.

2. Sustenance and Shelter

The maxim of choosing the best certainly should be applied to one's sustenance in such bodily matters as food, drink, sleep, and the like.

But apply it with intelligence. The best food for you is what you find to be the most nutritious and palatable for yourself. It need not be the luxurious food of a *gourmet*, and it need not be the quantity of a glutton. Why eat Whitstable or Colchester oysters, Russian caviare, pâté de fois gras, or drink pink champagne, Château Yquem and Chartreuse, if such expensive and rich purchases suit neither your purse nor your stomach? Why smoke Havanas because they are fashionable if you really prefer an acrid Virginia cigarette or French *caporal*? Or why smoke if you really prefer not to smoke at all?

Better than luxurious and expensive feeding, have the more vulgar bread-and-cheese and beer, or the more austere biscuit and cold water——if you (and your stomach) prefer these. However, never be afraid of experimenting in food and drink. And, above all, never economise on food to the detriment of your health and pleasure. Good food, artistically cooked and served, can be, and naturally ought to be, one of the most frequent and major pleasures of life. It is folly to despise it or pretend superiority to the pleasures of the palate.

As to drink: people are fond of dictating what is best for others, as though an absolute standard existed. More pretentious hypocrisy is talked about vintage wines, for instance, than on most subjects. Fashion also plays a disproportionate part here. You may loathe cocktails, but if "cocktail-parties" are fashionable everyone is popularly supposed to enjoy them. Similarly, when "sherry-parties" are fashionable, everyone is supposed to delight in drinking several glasses of cheap sherry before a meal—though to some stomachs and palates nothing can be more horrible! There are people (otherwise sensible) who think you eccentric or posing or superior, if you detest whisky or gin, and regard a teetotaller, by taste, as a slur on themselves or a spoil-sport. Alcohol in the year of our Lord 1954 is regarded as the only liquid in which one may drink another's health.

There is great pleasure in the best wines for many people. There is none for others. Many an individual prefers whisky or brandy, or even beer. Some, especially, I have noticed, if they are avid sweet-eaters, really care nothing for any kind of alcohol at all, and even perhaps rather dislike it. But the usual run of people who do like alcohol will simply not believe that it is possible for anyone to detest it who is not a propagandist-teetotaller, which is an example of current cant.

What drink is best for you? On the plain simple answer to that question (which none but you should be allowed to answer) depends what you should do in this regard. Do not lose sight of the fact that alcoholic drink is not the only dangerous drink when consumed too immoderately or frequently. Coffee, I repeat, killed the great Balzac. Over-strong, over-stewed, and too frequent cups of tea, "the cups that cheer but not inebriate," can be really harmful to the digestion. And many so-called "soft drinks" have deleterious ingredients. Nor are unboiled milk and unsterilised water always safe.

Without fearing reasonable risks, it is wise to take equally reasonable precautions. Never risk polluted food or drink, or even suspected food or drink. The stomach is a revengeful organ and punishes indiscretions sooner or later.

Moderation and prudence over food and drink are rules of safety, pleasure, and good-health.

Earnest people are very apt to economise rather on food than on clothing or shelter because such economies are more private than the others. Extravagance which you cannot afford is as much to be deprecated upon food as upon other items of expenditure, but it is folly to injure health and limit enjoyment, by economy on food. There are many obvious directions in which it is wiser to economise if economy is necessary.

Of shelter, it is curious to have to say that you will have the greatest difficulty in applying the maxim: "Choose the best". Which is the best: a palace or a cottage, a house in the country, a flat in town, or an hotel suite? What is best for one is not best for another. Here there is no absolute standard.

Even when you have decided on (say) a country-house or town-flat, the rule of "the best" may mean a different thing for me or for you. One may desire proximity to a railway-station; another may be very ready to sacrifice that to a picturesque setting. To one, a garage is a *sine qua non*; to another, a garden. Instances could be multiplied.

"It depends," as the late philosopher, Dr. Joad, used to be so fond of saying on the wireless, "on what you mean by the best." And, as usual in life, the emphasis is on the word "You".

Comfort and utility for one's purposes are perhaps a rule applicable to all choices of a home. Some people, and I will not say that they are wrong, put special emphasis on one room, a workshop, a study, a boudoir, or a bedroom, or even a bathroom.

Whatever individual desire may lead you to do regarding this emphasis, I would urge you to take some special care of your bedroom. You spend a third, or thereabouts, of your life in bed. Considering this fact, it is worth a special effort to be healthy, warm and comfortable there. On the quality of your sleep, too, depends much of your health and efficiency both in livelihood and leisure.

As to clothing, the importance to you in others' eyes of clean, neat, suitable clothing, needs no stressing. The best fabrics, the best workmanship, are expensive at first glance, but they more than repay their cost in appearance, wear, satisfaction, and in durability. Learn, too, to take care of your good clothes—a lesson male childhood and youth are too little taught.

Shoes in trees, coats on hangers, and pressed trousers, are worth the trifling extra trouble each night. Women in general take good care of their clothes, and are not as heedless as the male.

As to the wearing quality and value of good clothes, some concrete examples may speak convincingly from experience. Twelve years ago I had a pair of crocodile shoes hand-made to measure for £10. And worn frequently during that period, they are serviceable and good-looking to-day. "Yes," said their maker, with a sigh, as he inspected them recently. "And if you go on taking good care of them, they'll last you another twenty years or more. The same shoes to-day would cost you £25, hand-made to measure, but you won't want another pair." And I am able to look at my vicuña waistcoat, which cost me a fiver seven years ago, and which would cost £20 today, which has been worn every winter since then and which shows no sign of wear. It will probably keep me warm for life, for the tailor of it has a customer who still takes pride in the vicuña overcoat made for him 32 years ago.

Such "bests" as these are good enough for life, you must agree.

3. The Best for the Mind

Of course it is not less true that the "best" rule applies equally, if not more, to the things of the mind than to things of, and for, the body.

The best literature, journalism, plays, pictures, paintings, music, sculpture, architecture, radio and television, the treasures of the world and man's mind, are available for you. In these ask always: "What *is* the best?" Insist at any rate on trying how you like the reputed best.

But if you do not care for such "bests" as (say) Shakespeare in reading, Beethoven in music, or Michel Angelo in sculpture, after a fair trial of them, reluctantly conclude that they are not the best for you whatever they may be for the rest of the world.

The world may acclaim the strawberry as "the best berry God ever made", but if strawberries make you positively ill, as they do people allergic to them in a surprising number of cases, strawberries are better eschewed instead of being chewed by you. In some matters, what is best is a matter of taste, opinion, and idiosyncrasy. You may respect the received opinion of the cultured over the generations and yet be unable to accept it for your own case.

Do not conform from motives of snobbish deference. On the other hand, there is no need to flout received opinion. It is a high blunder in life to spend time on what has neither message nor meaning for you, or what bores and irritates when it exists for enjoyment and pleasure, as all art, music, literature, and indeed all culture, does.

We can finalise this chapter in one sentence: "In the practical business of living, choose and cleave to the best in everything, remembering that the best in this connection means the best for you."

CHAPTER XI

LIVING THE MULTIPLE LIFE

1. Concerning Experience

SHAKESPEARE tells us that "one man in his time plays many parts", beginning with the babe "mewling and puking in its nurse's arms" on the stage of this mortal life.

True enough, good Master Shakespeare. And your rich phraseology has lent glitter and splendour to that drab commonplace fact, already familiar to us all. But such parts as you depict, from infancy to old age, are played by mankind involuntarily.

What of the voluntary *rôles* we play upon the stage of this terrestial globe? Here, too, surely can be, and ought to be, multiplicity of parts if we are to lead the richest and fullest possible life.

Experience of life indeed can be hardly too varied. This we instinctively recognise in our attempts to widen the gambit of our ordinary routine-experience by recourse to books, newspapers, conversations, travel, films, radio, and television, and such-like extensions of experience. Yet, at best, many of these are second-hand experiences: they are not so much things experienced as others' experiences transmitted to, and received by, us at second-hand. They are a poor substitute for personal actual experience;

indeed, no more than a sort of reflection of the actual personal experience of other people.

Indeed, in spite of our arid longing for new and more thrilling experiences than those met with in our daily existence (which in modern sedentary or manual avocations is often exceedingly humdrum) we sink all too readily into rut and routine.

Being children of habit, and use-and-wont, as already noted, we therefore tend to keep strictly to the well-trodden paths with eyes fixed steadily upon the narrow ribbon of our way from cradle to grave. We ignore the rich meadows with their flora and fauna, lying on each side of the well-worn beaten track.

Not being adventurous, we do not have adventures. For "adventures are to the adventurous" as Disraeli said. Yet it is experience, first-hand personal experience, that teaches better than anything else; that enriches one's nature; that makes life interesting, colourful, and significant. If you want to live vitally and vividly, you must feed your inner self upon the the riches of the outer world.

Seek experiences of all kinds. Go everywhere and see everything. Talk with everyone. Be curious and satisfy your curiosities. Know how others live, the rich no less than the poor. Keep your eyes and ears open. Then you will not fail to be interested and enjoy yourself.

Do not confine yourself to conventional entertainments. See life as it is lived.

Suppose you live in London. Then ask yourself whether you have ever visited (a) a Cathedral service,

Anglican, Roman, and Greek; (b) a spiritualistic séance; (c) a Salvation Army revivalist meeting; (d) a Mohammedan mosque service; (e) a low-class "doss-house"; (f) a West-End luxury hotel; (g) a night-club; (h) an art-collection, like the National or Tate, Gallery; (i) the incomparable British Museum or any other of its kind; (j) a brewery at work; (k) a factory in full swing; (l) a nursery-garden; (m) a departmental-store both as a shopper and a visitor shown behind the scenes; (n) a street-market such as Petticoat Lane or the Caledonian Market; (o) a hospital (not as an inmate) but as a visitor or enquirer; (p) a prison (in a similar capacity as to a hospital); (q) a Magistrates' Court; (r) the High Court of Justice; (s) the Old Bailey (with a trial in progress); (t) a Government Department in Whitehall; (u) a Town Hall (to look at local Government); (v) the Royal Academy; (w) Service collections such as those at Greenwich or Whitehall; (x) Scotland Yard (to be shown round); (y) a City Livery Company's Hall; and (z) the House of Commons or the House of Lords (at work).

You see in this list of suggestions I have exhausted the alphabet. But I have not exhausted a tenth of the spectacles which an ordinary London-dweller (say) might enjoy, freely and without tax. All are worth trying. Some you will wish to repeat; some not. Some will give you permanent gain; some undoubtedly will be useless to you. A country-dweller could draw up an equivalent list.

Again, if you are a Londoner, I need hardly urge you to watch out for special exhibitions, concerts,

F

theatrical performances, public events of an exceptional character, that you may like to go and see.

All these experiences are of a quasi-domestic character, inasmuch as one leaves home only for a few hours to enjoy them. In addition, there is the exploration of the country round your home, both near and far. It is both shameful and shocking how little we British know of our own islands. Notice I use the plural.

Travel—which should mean living the foreign life abroad has already been advocated. Until one is old, one can hardly have enough of it in the intervals of a working life.

Take full advantage of the few—the all too few— good years of life, remembering that extreme infancy and extreme old age profit you far less than the years between, in the very nature of things.

2. Concerning "Estates" of Life

Experience does not consist merely of the things dealt with above. There is such a thing as what the Book of Common Prayer calls "estates of life".

Marriage is one such estate of life. So is fatherhood or motherhood. Grand-parentage (a foolishly neglected estate) is yet another. These are natural estates. Also there are artificial "estates of life" which you may take upon yourself, other than your ordinary avocations, such as becoming a Councillor, an M.P., or entering public or semi-public life in some form or another.

That great lawyer, famous for common-sense and sound judgment, of the time of Queen Elizabeth the

First, John Selden, had a great saying upon Marriage. He declared: "Marriage is a desperate thing".

And so, indeed, it may be, as Divorce Court stories show, and as our knowledge of the world tells us. A modern lawyer, instructed to give "counsel's opinion" as to whether or not a partnership or contract should be entered into on the terms of the marriage-tie would unhesitatingly advise against it. He would say, from the point of view of a lawyer and a man of affairs, that the risk was too great; the security too little; the obligations too vague, uncertain, and ill-defined; the consideration insufficient; and the mere verbal covenants not enough. Certainly he would want to draw up a stringently worded document, and have both parties sign it, at the very least.

Yet, desperate as marriage may be, from a legal or business standpoint, the majority of mankind ignore this side of it and enter upon it light-heartedly enough. Nature sees to that. The strongest natural instinct—that of reproduction and perpetuation of the species—is at work here.

But if man or woman must marry, they can at least exercise some care and judgment, even though the choice, since natural preference comes so strongly into play, is not entirely free and unfettered. The god or goddess you fall in love with can be inspected for feet of clay. Because the heart rules, the head need not altogether be left out.

Sir Walter Raleigh of Tudor days put it well in some advice to his son: "Though thou cans't not forbear to love" he told him, "yet thou cans't forbear to link". An attractive sweetheart may make a very bad marital partner. Marriage, it should never be forgotten, is a lengthy, day-by-day, all-day-and-every-day business. You should choose a spouse as you choose a garment, partly for wearing-quality. The choice made by youth at twenty may have to serve old age at seventy—as well as all the half-century between.

It is well, therefore, to abstain from marriage until one knows a good deal about one's fellow-creatures, especially those of the opposite sex, and until one's judgment is mature.

The main feature of marriage is often forgotten. It is not sex, vitally important though that is. It is not even affection or love. It is the fact that in marriage one's life is no longer entirely one's own. It is a shared existence through the identification of marriage with cohabitation. Therefore compatability, or harmony of temperament, is of the very first importance. Neither love nor sex, nor both, will ensure happiness if there is incompatibility, a disharmony of temperament, between the joint-harnessed pair. Indeed these concomitants of marriage will, in that case, only intensify the tragedy.

No one saw this great truth more clearly, or expressed it more vehemently and eloquently, than the great poet and Englishman, John Milton, whose tractates on what he called "the godly doctrine and discipline of divorce . . . restored to the good of both sexes from the bondage of Canon Law and other mistakes", are largely forgotten, except by scholars, students, and literary men. The Western Churches, with their over-emphasis on adultery and the physical side of marriage, with what Gibbon, the historian, called "the ambiguous word of Christ", are responsible for a general forgetfulness of the real spirit that makes marriage an endurable life-long contract.

The teaching of the small Cromwellian sect of "Miltonists or Divorcers" is not so much discredited as ignored, because organised Western religion is committed to regarding divorce as an evil, and the subsistence of a bad, or even tragic, marriage as a better thing.

Even in Stuart days, at first Milton regarded himself as the sole advocate of a discountenanced truth, exercising the right and duty of an instructed Christian.

Yet Milton, with his fierce insistence that the soul's harmony with twin-soul, and not the body, was what mattered most, had grasped the real truth about marriage.

Religion teaches us to regard marriage as a mystical sacrament. But there are other sides to it. From the worldly point of view, it is both a partnership and a contract with duties and obligations to be faced. If you marry, therefore, it is wise to look at every aspect of the relation—and see that the other party does so, too.

Another change of estate comes when the married person becomes a parent. If you believe in life (and if you did not, you would not be reading this book), you will be all for parentage. Children are a joy and solace and source of satisfaction, though seldom

indeed do they fulfil all their parents' hopes and
wishes. Nevertheless, they satisfy even when they are
unsatisfactory and disappointing and ungrateful,
inasmuch as one feels that one has not entirely died
in one's personal death. One has handed on the torch
of life. In this at least one has fulfilled the mysterious
purpose of Life and Nature, however one may have
failed or fallen short in one's personal possibilities
and achievements.

Even from a baser standpoint, children in the
modern world are a form of wealth—though for many
years they cost money and add to one's expenses and
anxieties. A barren marriage is tolerated and even
regarded as satisfactory by many Western couples—
but essentially it is not an entirely satisfactory affair.

A couple may be united to each other by nature in
all or almost all points that matter. But such cases
are rare good fortune; and the odds are heavily
against this. Fortunately, harmony, and even unity,
may be attained, even where this is not so, by a
process of delicate adjustments, or, as it is sometimes
called, "give-and-take". Compromise and a willing-
ness to adjust relationship, diplomacy, tact, goodwill,
and consideration, are as necessary in marriage as in
other and less intimate relationships in life. Parentage
also calls for qualities of sensitiveness and understanding. Children may be born, but good fathers
and mothers are made.

Yet another "estate of life" worth considering is
that of godparent. This relation of godparent and
godchild has largely become degraded into a merely
nominal and conventional one in modern times. But

the artist in life will not be content with mere attendance at a font for baptismal purposes and the gift of a mere christening-mug or similar present. He, or she, will cultivate lifelong, or certainly youth-long relations with the godchild, to the friendship and enrichment of both their lives.

On this subject I can speak from personal experience. One of my most satisfying lifelong relationships has been with a godson, whose character, progress, and friendship have delighted me throughout a quarter-of-a-century, and promise to do so to the end.

3. Concerning Friends, Animals and Plants

It is inevitable that the many-sided man or woman leading a full subjective and objective life, will have a large circle of acquaintances. Amongst these he will have circles of friends, some transitory and more or less distant, others permanent and close.

These last will inevitably be few.

Real friends are precious indeed. "Grapple them to thy soul with hoops of steel" advised Shakespeare's Polonius, and the old worldling was right. But to make and retain friends, you yourself must show friendship, and keep your friendship in constant repair.

A real friend is one in whom you can entirely confide and with whom you can be your sincere self.

We all, though sometimes it is somewhat late in life, learn the worth and rarity of true friends. A friend may be nearer and dearer than a blood-brother, as in the classic cases of Saul and Jonathan, and Damon and Pythias. But beware of giving your close friendship in an unworthy direction. A friend should be tried, tested, and true—or no intimate friend at all.

But do not forget that this world is not a world of human beings alone. Humbler forms of life than the human are not to be disregarded, or much mental and spiritual wealth will be lost. Not to have known intimately a cat or a dog, a rabbit or a bird, or some other form of pet, is to have missed a treasure and a pleasure in life. Also you may find satisfactory relations in cultivating and caring for the living plants in garden or countryside, or both, even though you are not a passionate and specialised nature-lover or horticultural enthusiast.

These are all a part of the richness and diversity of earthly life, often forgotten by the undiscerning and conventionalized modern mind. Be wiser than the generality in this regard and your wisdom will have its reward.

I had much pleasure in the conversation of a small boy who used to talk thus: "A friend of mine who is a horse calls at our house every day. He brings the milkman and our milk, and I always go out for a chat and to give him his lump of sugar. He's a most grateful and thoughtful fellow and generally leaves his manure for our garden just outside the house. Another friend of mine, who is a grey squirrel by nature, used to meet me in the garden for his nuts and bread and milk. And then I was ill once and couldn't go out with his rations, the squirrel came straight into the kitchen to find out where I was . . ."

That little boy had certainly the right idea of making friends with animals. His mother summed up the effect upon him: "I never knew such a happy and serene little boy as John. This communion with animals certainly keeps him in a state of bliss all day long."

4. Concerning the Inanimate World

Nor should one neglect to explore the inanimate world, whether of Nature's or man's production.

It may be that your nature is objective rather than subjective. You may have an undiscovered taste for science or mechanics. Rocks and stones (dull, lifeless, speechless things to some of us) may fascinate and enthral you. Or tinkering with the mechanism of clocks, locks, motors, planes, or electric or other gadgets, may fill you with interest and delight. Explore these possibilities. Find yourself out. People's minds, like their bodies, differ in nature, and many men and women have failed to discover their true *métier* and their real taste because they have been too apathetic and inert to explore the whole rich field of our diversified existence.

What a mistake to miss one's way in life from self-imposed indifference, ignorance, and inertia! This is the medieval Church's sin of "accidie"—now largely forgotten even by ecclesiastics and theologians. It is also the Buddhist sin of "unawareness" or "stupidity". Certainly on any showing it is a crime against oneself and the gift of life: the burial of one's talent in a napkin instead of using it.

People sometimes condemn a man for "leading a

double life". Such a man is generally a bigamist. There is a sense, a true sense, in which men or women can be condemned for leading only a single life—which is not to be confused with a single-hearted life, a very different and noble thing. We all ought to lead not one life but multiple lives; not discordant in nature but consistent with the united integral personality of oneself.

You perceive what this means from the contents of this chapter. It means a selected, but infinite variety, of relationships between your own life and all other modes and manifestations of existence, whether animate or inanimate.

Which last sentence, perhaps, is a sufficient summing-up of this chapter.

CHAPTER XII

SELFISHNESS AND SELFLESSNESS

1. Claims to be Admitted or Resisted

ON seeing the title of this chapter, you will probably exclaim: "Now for a sermon. I know what's coming. Heard it all before! Be unselfish. You needn't preach that. I agree. Selfishness is the very devil, the Father of all Evil to which we are all prone; and selflessness is fine, heroic, the ideal to aim at."

Not so. At any rate not quite so. You had better read on, unafraid and unanticipative of the usual platitudes, and *clichés*, on this subject.

Already you are aware that contrary to most instructions, I have stressed the Duty towards Yourself. This is a world of claims, as directly you leave the dependence of childhood and youth behind you will soon learn. Claims upon your time (which is your life's current banking-account). Claims upon your money (which is your life's deposit banking-account). Claims upon your allegiance. Claims voluntary (like adjurations to support and subscribe to this and that aggregation of your fellows) and involuntary (like demands for income-tax, rates, national service, and the like).

There is no end to them as life goes on, especially

if you attain any position of standing, respectability, and influence.

Some of these claims obviously must be conceded. Some may be, or may be not, conceded at your pleasure. Others ought to be resisted. Indeed, if you do not resist the vast majority of them, you will, like the married man not knowing Bunbury in Oscar Wilde's play, *The Importance of Being Earnest*, have "a very tedious time of it". You will hardly have any time or money or life-for-yourself at all.

We are bidden "to love our neighbour as ourselves". But this does not say we should not love ourselves. Indeed, this command postulates that we do. Nor does it say that we should love (or treat) our neighbour, or an aggregate of neighbours, better than ourselves.

Self-regard, which many people denounce under the name of selfishness, is not entirely to be reprobated. Rather is it, in sensible moderation, to be praised and fostered. Unfortunately most people talk such hypocrisy about selfishness and unselfishness, as though one were unmitigated vice and the other spotless and unsullied virtue, that the truth is obscured.

Truth, however, is never pure, being usually mixed with a modicum of falsity if not falsehood. Nor is it simple. Rather is it complex and difficult of exact ascertainment and definition. It is so, here.

Think a little on the subject of selfishness and its opposite. When Bernard Shaw in youth stuck to his unremunerative writing and sponged for livelihood on the hard-working music-teacher, his own mother, he was strongly denounced at the time by a family observer for his selfish and wicked behaviour. (He respected his denouncer but scorned the denunciation.) Yet he was right, and his after-career proved it. Had he "unselfishly" given up his writing, taken a clerkship or other employment, kept his mother and himself, he would have done wrong, and he knew this very well, though others neither saw nor believed it.

Unselfishness, even true and admirable unselfishness, can do harm, sometimes. Children, as we are all well aware, can be spoiled by parents' excessive unselfishness. Emerson, the American philosopher, has well pointed out "The hand that feeds us is in great danger of being bitten". This is not mere cynicism. It is a sad, human, truth, that life demonstrates only too often and too sickeningly.

There are many *dicta* to similar effect. "Gratitude has a short memory: hope, a long one" will serve to illustrate proverbs to similar effect in all languages and current amongst all the peoples of the earth.

So do not let us unthinkingly subscribe to the conventional and artificial view of selfishness and selflessness. This view, as the examples cited above show, is not "the truth, the whole truth, and nothing but the truth" about this subject. It is well to remember that, as Herbert Spencer grandiloquently put it: "In all verity there is a nucleus of falsity".

Surely it follows, then, that we should not be afraid of revising the current ideas. (Ideas are seldom for all time: they may last an age and then wear out or rust out.) It may be both refreshing and constructive to consider the opposite idea (it usually is, by the way) namely, that selfishness is to be commended. Nowhere have I found it more trenchantly expressed than in the philosophy of the German Max Stirner, the precursor of the more celebrated Nietzsche (now less read and considered than his genius deserves).

Max Stirner wrote a book called *The Ego and His Own*, which had some vogue amongst the learned. Here are some of his maxims, which give *in petto* a very fair idea of his theme—the importance of the ego in human life:

"Nothing is more to me than myself."

(Nakedly expressed like that, this seems no more than individualistic anarchism. But if you reflect that if you do not exist, the whole world, nay the whole universe, and its contents, have, for you, no existence, you begin to see that there is more profundity and truth in this bald and brutal assertion than you perhaps thought.)

"My concern is myself."

"What I want I must have, and will procure."

"I must realise value from myself."

"Unlike what is demanded of us, God makes no alien cause his own, serves no higher person, and satisfies only Himself."

Stirner's utterances cannot be regarded as the acme of nobility, and one can easily have too much of their Teutonic self-assertiveness. But as an antidote to much of the current Anglo-Saxon hypocrisy upon unselfishness, they have their usefulness in restoring the balance between egoism and sentimentality.

Without derogating from our duties to our fellows, it can be said plainly (and it requires to be said) that self-regard, self-preservation, and self-aggrandisement, are duties and not mere vices. Observe how mankind, while deprecating and decrying these mental attitudes, consistently bases its policy and actions upon them. It is now as of old: when the able Machiavelli plainly stated in cold print the philosophy of force and fraud on which every State in Italy, and indeed in Europe, acted consistently, that great writer was instantly traduced as a scoundrel and his very name, Machiavelli, became a hissing and a reproach and a symbol of all diabolism.

An academic contest between selfishness and unselfishness as a matter of debate, gets nowhere. What is important in human living is to strike the sensible balance between them; so far as may be, and not to be the prey of mental illusions, or the dupe of men's speeches or writings glorifying the denigration of the self.

It is with the self, and not the not-self, that you have to deal in struggling against the phenomena prescribed by life. To that extent, Stirner's emphasis on the self is right.

2. Of the Intensified Self.

Can the self increase itself? Can the self be intensified? Already in the chapter on personality, we have seen that there are natural limitations but that there can be extensions by mental effort.

What are the laws of mental hygiene applicable to

yourself? Most people are completely in the dark as to their mental as well as physical powers.

Find out by testing it, under what conditions your brain works best, easiest, and most willingly. It may be an hour on rising in the morning. It may be under the stimulus of artificial light in the quietude of night.

For how long can you work mentally to the best advantage? Discover the maximum working-power of your mind, which is as real and ascertainable as the horse-power of your car. Every accomplished task increases our powers and also our sense of power. The pleasure arising from this enhanced sense of power is a mental purification; a step towards better mental hygiene.

Emotion comes in here. People and things arouse agreeable or disagreeable feelings. But it is in the power of the governing part of your mind to encourage the agreeable and suppress the disagreeable feeling. Do not waste feeling, passion and mental power upon objects unworthy of them. We are all too apt to do this—in spite of our wiser selves.

One selfish duty we owe ourselves is never to worry. Not even about *anything*. Compel the mind to switch off as you switch off an electric light. Deny existence (by putting the mind deliberately on to something else) to perpetually recurring trains of thought. Practice the device of refusing consideration to small worries.

Yet another duty (both selfish and unselfish) is the control of the passions. This is a matter of will-power, constantly and habitually exercised towards this end.

Self-esteem is a further selfish duty to be cultivated.

According to Pythagoras, we should "respect ourselves above all". And even that eminent Christian, John Milton, tells us that "Nothing profits more than self-esteem founded on just and right". It has been called the elixir of the soul. Build it up by small successes which have a tonic and bracing effect on the whole mind.

It is this self-esteem, backed by an instinct towards self-preservation, which enables you to resist the fearful weight of the world, ever-pressing upon the individual with fears that darken our lives, and lie, like lead, upon the free-working of our mental powers. The innumerable commandments laid on modern men and women by laws, bye-laws, police regulations, conventions, rules of morality, partial physical breakdowns, and the rest, would be unendurable but for the detachment from them in our inner selves, and our own self-confidence.

On this great question of self, remember a great saying by the Victorian Samuel Butler: "The laws of God are the laws of our own well-being."

And what are those "laws of God", little preached but surely realised by all who think? Do you imagine that a beneficient Deity desires your ill-health, your folly, your ill-nature, your poverty and misery? Then is it not common-sense to assert that the Divine law includes "Thou shalt have as much good health as may be, as much good sense as may be, as much experience, kindliness of nature, and worldly goods, as may be necessary for your comfortable passage throughout life"?

Not against this, but with this, goes the often-preached Duty to God and Neighbour. A restrained selfishness or egoism is as necessary as the unrestrained unselfishness or altruism which is the cement of social life and which may rise, on occasion, to heroic or sublime heights. You are made for individual, as well as for social, ends.

It follows, surely, that self-education (as distinct from scholastic and formal education) is both a selfish and an unselfish duty. It, at one and the same time, fits you to stand alone and to fit into the milieu of your fellows. This whole book deals with the subject of self-education to the widest possible degree, but you may find inspiration and value in this task by considering some more Butlerian aphorisms.

"Don't 'learn to do' (anything): Learn by doing." (This, indeed, is how one learns most swiftly and effectively).

"Let subjects choose you: not you them." (Accordingly, you will follow your bent, the most fruitful way of progress and success.)

"Only learn when not knowing comes to be a nuisance to you." (In this way the clogging and cluttering-up that makes so many minds ineffective, is avoided, and you learn swiftly and surely what is needful under the pressure of necessity.)

Perhaps on the subject of self-education one should glance at the subject of books. For books hypnotise the youthful mind, and not youthful minds only. It is possible to exaggerate the virtues of much reading, for too much is as bad as too little. A very conservative estimate puts the number of printed books at 5 million separate and distinct treatises. In 50 years of reading-life, at a good average rate of reading, you would read 1,250. That is about one in every 3,600 books.

So the question you ought to put to yourself before engaging in the reading of any book is: "Is this book one in 3,600? Otherwise I could read a better one, and the worse excludes my reading the better."

But it is far more important to successful living to "read" oneself and other people than to read books. Books are a valuable help. Nothing more. And unless you read to the purpose and assimilate, you had better not soak your mind too much in print. With more advantage you might use that mind in thinking.

It is a horrible fact that schools and universities teach everything but the work of thinking—the prime duty of the individual. Students are taught merely to know, to remember, and to believe. Their heads are turned into warehouses rather than workshops. They have learned neither the mental work of original observation nor individual introspection—and therefore they tend to lead secondhand lives, and not their own. They are incomplete minds and therefore incomplete human beings, cursed with a pseudo-education instead of an education in life.

This inadequacy of formal education makes one realise the vital necessity of self-education and education in life.

True, self-gained education at any rate will prevent one from falling a victim to the mental climate of contemporary thought which seeks so persistently to confuse and confound the individual with the herd-aggregate or the community. This sublimation of self, which makes a person no longer a person in himself but a trades-unionist, a nationalist, a citizen of a coming World-State, in short, a grouping, can be bought too dearly if the price is to be an annihilation instead of an extension of the individual personality. The totalitarian horrors to which this philosophy of selflessness may give rise, have been imaginatively pictured by Aldous Huxley in *Brave New World*, and in George Orwell's *Nineteen Eighty-four*. The motto "I am you and you are I" is a false and misleading superstitition, for we cannot be our neighbour nor can he be us.

Then what, it may be asked, of the unselfish team-spirit, of the corporative and co-operative spirit of *esprit-de-corps*, loyalty, patriotism, and the like civic virtues? These are excellent in their times and places. Men and women are made for co-operation, as hands and brain, teeth and tongue, and other parts of the one body for men and women are units of humanity. They are, moreover, social and gregarious animals. In a million instances it is necessary, desirable, and imperative that aggregates of humanity should act, and even think and speak, together, and they do, as everyone knows.

However, the modern spirit is heavily to over-emphasise this aspect of things. Salvation is popularly supposed to lie in communistic or communal effort by committees, groups, nations, and mankind, and what is called their "solidarity". To an extent this is of course true; and we all avail ourselves of the weight attaching to organised numbers as a means to individual and social progress. The "get-together" attitude is natural and productive of much good. There are notable achievements which can only be accomplished by the goodwill, and with the assistance of, one's fellows.

But there is a discernible limit to all this. We are born as solitary individuals, even in a twin-birth, and we must die as solitary individuals. No "solidarity" with our fellows avails in the end. Nor does it avail us entirely in our progress through life. Each of us—even the most corporative and team-minded—perforce lives most in a world of himself and his own, which is not the interior world of any other human being. There is no escape from these facts. Ignoring them, they will not ignore us but will continue to exist as verities and realities of human life as long as men endure. We are conditioned by these unsurmountable solitudes which our nearest and dearest cannot share.

What comfort is there when one inevitably grows old, and perhaps decrepit, and faces the inevitability of death? Is it as terrifying as depicted in Rochester's stark lines:

> "Then Old Age and Experience hand-in-hand
> Lead him to death and make him understand
> After a time so painful and so long
> That all his life he has been in the wrong.
> Huddled in dirt the reasoning engine lies
> That was so proud, so witty and so wise."

A frightful picture indeed, as horrible as anything depicted by the Spanish painter Goya! But in leading us to death, as they indeed must, Old Age and Experience may make us understand something better than our failures, faults, and frailties. These can hardly be the whole story of even the worst and most unfortunate of us. There is more in the poorest life than Rochester depicts.

If we can say, in spite of all our sins and short-comings, "I have fulfilled my function in the world. I have been myself and led my own life, cultivating my garden, and in so doing have left the world no worse but even perhaps a trifle better for my having been in it, and I have handed on the torch", we can face our personal end with equanimity when Nature throws us into her dust-bin. We may then perhaps feel, with John Bunyan's Christian, coming to the deep waters: "Death where is thy sting, Grave where is Thy Victory?"

But whether the trumpets do, or do not, sound for us "on the other side", we triumph in true immortality since we can say, as he said: "My sword I leave to him who shall succeed me in my pilgrimage, and my courage and skill to him that can get it."

With such last words as those we may well make a good end.

CHAPTER XIII

TEACHERS OF HOW TO LIVE

IN some sense, all religions and all philosophies, as we have seen, produce exponents of their creeds who essay to teach us how best to live. From all of such spirits, one can profitably learn of life, present or to come, in its broadest and highest sense.

But for the day-by-day business of practical living here and now in this world, of learning self-wisdom and worldly wisdom, of cultivating self-development and self-enlightenment, as distinct from the highest wisdom taught by religions and philosophies, one must go to teachers of lesser terrestial, as opposed to celestial, scope.

One of the greatest and best of these is the Roman Emperor, Marcus Aurelius, whose famous *Meditations* repay one's own meditation. This ancient book is one not to be merely read but pondered over and re-read again and again.

As a literary work, this justly celebrated book has grave faults. It is disjointed and fragmentary and repetitive. Its text is corrupt in places. It is not a unity. It is far from artistic. But as a sound practical guide to living sanely and satisfactorily, and in the high nobility of its outlook upon self and one's fellow-men, it ranks in the very highest class, above the moral discourses of Epictetus, which also may be recommended.

Marcus Aurelius Antoninus, who lived over 1800 years ago, had a noble mind, as his writings testify. His book is considered one of the most precious legacies of antiquity, and John Stuart Mill thought it almost equal in elevation to Christ's Sermon on the Mount.

Above all things, Aurelius is practical in his teaching, and hence his inclusion here. The goal of life, he says, is not happiness but equanimity, or tranquillity of spirit.

This can be attained only by "living comformably to nature"—that is to say, one's whole nature. As a means to that we must cultivate the four chief virtues of life, which are:

Wisdom or the Knowledge of Good and Evil.
Justice or the giving of every man his due.
Fortitude or the enduring of life's labour and pain.
Temperance or moderation in all things.

We must govern ourselves by the divinity of rational principle within. We must live as a social animal, but yet at times as on a mountain. We must not be displeased or afflicted by anything that happens, since all that happens is in accordance with nature and the scheme of things. In obedience to the law of our higher nature, we can regard both life and death with serenity and calm.

This brief and imperfect summary of Aurelian teaching gives no idea of the exquisite charm and tenderness with which the thinker expresses his ideas, so pure, sincere, unaffected and free from all taint of man's baser self.

Four good translations into English are those of George Long, G. H. Rendall, J. Jackson, and Jeremy Collier. Any of these will serve the English reader well.

From an ancient Roman Emperor to a Renaissance Spanish Jesuit, is a far cry, and it is a descent from Aurelian sublimity to Gracián casuistry. But *The Art of Worldly Wisdom* of Gracián, translated into English by Joseph Jacobs, should not be neglected by students in the art of living.

Balthasar Gracián y Morales (1601-1658) is little known in England but is well worth knowing. He is an acute thinker and observer of the subjects of humanity and life, and Schopenhauer praised him highly. But Ticknor and the late John Morley denigrated him for many English readers with a few patronising words—but he will outlast Morley and Ticknor.

His Oracles are worldly wisdom *in excelsis*, full of Jesuitical subtlety, force, and good sense. Here are a few of his leading head-notes which give a quick and good idea of his cleverness:

"If you cannot clothe yourself in Lion's skin use a Fox's pelt."

"Neither belong entirely to Yourself nor to others."

"Find out each man's thumbscrew."

"Never take payment in politeness."

"Have a touch of the trader in you."

"Do pleasant things yourself, unpleasant things through others."

"Know how to take your own part."

"Do not show your wounded finger."

As an instance of his constant good sense, one may perhaps quote what he has to say upon the subject of "Never talk of yourself", a common mistake most of us make:

"You must either praise yourself, which is vain, or blame yourself, which is little-minded. It ill beseems him that speaks and ill pleases him which hears. And if you should avoid this in ordinary conversation, how much more in official matters, and above all in public speaking, where every appearance of unwisdom really is unwise . . ."

A much greater teacher of the art of "wisdom for a man's self", and equally astute, is the English Francis Bacon, who lived about the same time. Bacon's *Essays* are so well-known as only need to be mentioned here. Less well-known, but not less valuable, to the student of life and human nature, are his *Apophthegms*.

"Certainly they are of excellent use", as he, himself, suggests. He omitted "the dull and flat", and with Cicero called those he included "salt-pits" and most of them are salty indeed. But Lord Bacon, "the brightest, wisest, meanest, of mankind", according to Pope, never wearied of the subject of getting on in life. To that topic he recurred again and again. Sagacity and good sense on this subject mark his every utterance.

Here, for instance, are his general principles, from his *De Augmentis*. Neither exalted nor heroic, they

are of the world, worldly, and an epitome of the
wisdom that leads to worldly success:

1. Accustom your mind to judge the proportion
of things as they more or less conduce to your own
fortune or ends.

2. Never row against the stream.

3. Do not always wait for occasions but sometimes challenge and induce them.

4. Undertake nothing which of necessity takes up
a great quantity of time.

5. Imitate Nature, which does nothing in vain.
Mix and interlace your several kinds of business.
Nothing is more impolitic than to be entirely based
upon one action.

6. Always have a window open to fly out at, or a
secret door to retire by.

7. Love as if you were sometime to hate, and hate
as if you were sometime to love. This is the maxim of
Bias, not construed to any point of perfidiousness.

There is something repulsive about a number of
these maxims, and they remind us that crawling and
climbing are done in the same attitude. Nevertheless,
astuteness and fitness to their purpose are undeniable.

In Hanoverian days, the incomparable Earl of
Chesterfield, an ambassador, a minister, a Viceroy
of Ireland, and one of the most famous figures of his
day, wrote a series of private letters to his illegitimate
son, Philip Stanhope. They were never intended for
the public; they were intended to form one youthful
mind and heart in preparation for a brilliant career.
But the son died; the father died; and the son's widow
published.

The brilliance of these *Letters to His Son* made an instant sensation on cultivated people in England and on the Continent. Their substance was remarkable, the style enchanting and admirably suited to the matter. Dr. Johnson, who was ungrateful to Chesterfield for bounty which he regarded as insufficient, at first denigrated the *Letters* as teaching "the morals of a whore and the manners of a dancing master," but later grudingly joined the chorus of praise with Voltaire and the rest.

Now Lord Chesterfield had deeply and persistently studied his fellow-men. He knew the human heart and mind as few know it. In his *Letters*, he strove with unwearied labour and skill, to give that knowledge to a much-loved son whom he wished to perfect in knowledge of the world of men. In that one respect— knowledge of human nature—the *Letters* are brilliant indeed, and in that respect they never can be out-of-date, for human nature essentially does not change, though its outward expressions of itself alter much.

From the modern point of view, the great defect of the *Letters* is not the immorality and contempt of womanhood, with which they have been often reproached, so much as the absence of the scientific and economic outlook. Chesterfield's world is political and social. He was far from uninterested in the science or economics of his day, but in that day neither science nor economics had advanced to anything like their present paramount position.

The wit as well as the wisdom of Lord Chesterfield —probably the most-quoted man of his day next to Voltaire and Johnson—is proverbial. One could cite him interminably, but it may be more profitable to deal here with his leading ideas.

The art of life, according to Lord Chesterfield, lies in knowledge of the world, discernment of character, suppleness and versatility of a well-stocked mind, and elegancy of manners. Upon the last, as a passport to man's hearts and thence to their minds, he was especially insistent. We must "sacrifice to the Graces", and constantly study the art of pleasing, by engaging the eyes and soothing the ears. Mastery of temper; coolness of mind; serenity of countenance; grace and charm of manner; activity; diligence; order; method; despatch; the perfect control of oneself and command of others, were the lessons of this aristocrat. Vanity, he says, is the master-key of mankind, and people's regard is cheaply bought with small attentions and civilities.

You will discover more truth by your eyes than your ears. Make people like themselves better, and they will like you. Keep an open face but close thoughts. Never do nothing, and never spend a shilling or a moment without advantage. By application and care we may acquire almost anything except the poetic gift. But the air, the manner, the grace, the elegance, the style, is of transcendent importance in all we do or say—because the vulgar world is taken by appearances and not by realities, and all people have eyes and ears but very few have judgments.

The above, while not being entirely complete, will give a fairly full and entirely accurate idea of Lord Chesterfield's gospel. But it is no substitute for the pleasure and profit of reading his admirable *Letters*, in which his teaching is embedded.

From Chesterfield one comes to more modern times. In the days of Victoria, a prosaic book by Samuel Smiles, called *Self Help*, had a great vogue. It was believed to be instrumental in turning earnest young persons into wealthy and respectable successes in business. It was sneered at unjustly and went out of fashion, but its heavy emphasis was of course on livelihood rather than living. It is full of common-sense and worth some attention.

Coming to still later times, Arnold Bennett, the immortal author of that great picture of provincial life *The Old Wives Tale* (which posterity will treasure) wrote a number of pocket-philosophies, one of which, *How to Live on 24 Hours a Day*, sold more copies, as I have said, than any of his other books. These books can still be read with pleasure. I knew Bennett, a practising Aurelian and in many respects a striver after connoisseurship in life, as his writings show.

Another book, deserving of more attention than it has received, which consciously and perhaps rather too self-consciously and affectedly, aims direct at teaching how to live, is Sir James Yoxall's *Live and Learn*. It is rather pedagogic, but it is a sensible book in which a widely read artist in living shows how life can be made an artistic whole. It deserves more fame than it has attained.

Not only the books like those I have mentioned, which aim directly at the target on how to live, but books which incidentally deal with the subject, contain valuable sidelights in the art of living. Biographies and autobiographies are particularly rich in this sort of material; so too are collections of aphorisms such as Logan Pearsall Smith's *A Treasury of English Aphorisms*. Such autobiographies as Trollope's, and Somerset Maugham's *The Summing Up*, are examples of particularly valuable English authors' books of this kind—the latter being much the more useful of the two. Then, also, the French epigrammatists, like Rochefoucaulds, Vauvenargues, Chamfort, are rich in strong and even dazzling searchlights upon human life and human nature. These last indeed from this point of view cannot be too highly recommended for occasional reading.

Indeed, all literature, especially fiction in all its forms of poems, novels, plays, and short stories, which takes life for its province, is of concern to the students of life. But the last word, and the greatest on the subject, is that spoken to us by life in action, both in ourselves and in others. For it is in living to learn that we best learn to live.

THE END